LEHIGH VALLEY

LVMA

MUSIC AWARDS

12

3115 Tilghman Street, Allentown, PA 18104

610-437-5813 • www.docswestendmusic.com

Instruments • Lessons • Repairs • Band Instruments

 **Dedication**

This book is dedicated to those talented people who gave of themselves and persevered throughout the years to make the Lehigh Valley music and entertainment scene what is today.

Table of Contents

 A PERSONAL NOTE

Much of what you are about to see and read comes from personal experience, historical fact and contributions from performers, band members, members of the media, friends, fans and just plain folks who love music.

Having spent my entire adult life in the Lehigh Valley as part of the music business as a DJ in clubs and radio, club management, a promoter and on the board of directors of a state wide song-writers organization has allowed me to witness first-hand, history from a first person aspect.

From the early days as a DJ of a 100MW home radio station in my basement (some may call it a pirate station) to booking concerts and everything in between, it was an experience that made my life what it is today.

Having spent my early days as a gopher or house roadie at King Arthurs Court allowed me to see the emergence of some of the finest garage bands and talented performers that the Lehigh Valley had to offer. In the years of the early 70's, my talents as a House DJ for clubs enabled me to hear some of the best music around and meet those band members that I would call friends for years to come.

I must have played opposite at least 400 bands in my career as a DJ at clubs like Odysseus/Scarlett O'Haras, The Rock Palace/Music Factory, Hideaway Park and a host of others. The highlight of my DJ career was the Studio 13 Show that I did from Castle Garden in Dorney Park live on WKAP AM 1320 during 1979. I would play to approx. 2000 people nightly and being live, a lot more listeners felt the experience.

My foray into national shows started with Makoul Productions in 1976 as an associate of Tom Makoul working with such acts as Supertramp, Jeff Beck, Rush, John- Luc Ponty and others. In March 1983, as a fledgling promoter, I booked The Romantics, Single Bullet Theory and Crisis at Muhlenberg College. The show gave me the experience that I would need in the future.

In September of 1983, I became a member of PASCAL, The PA. Assoc of Songwriters, Composers & Lyricists and later would be a VP/Secretary and member of their Board of Directors. This phase started my commitment to original music and allowed me to work with many talented individuals.

The Airport Music Hall and Club PASCAL was one of those times in my life where creativity would be paramount.

The start of this venue came the week after Castle Garden burned to the ground and left rock band Magnum without a place to do their annual Thanksgiving Eve show. John Havassy, PAS-

CAL and I got together with the principals involved and offered The Airport Bingo Hall as the place for the group to play. This first night, the place was named The Airport Arena, which would give birth to the evolution of The Airport Music Hall and its sister, Club PASCAL.

I became involved with The Allentown Council of Youth and restarted the outdoor concerts in Lehigh Parkway and Cedar Beach Park. I also became involved with The Allentown Fair and the Farmerama Theater. PASCAL would run a stage for a Battle of the Bands for the fair during those years. This also allowed me to meet some of the top entertainers of the day.

In the 90's, I returned to radio and club DJ work working for local and regional clubs, radio stations WGPA and WLEV until my retirement in 1997 from the business.

I continued being a spectator of music and would go to shows ranging from local to national acts for years to come and sometimes lend my expertise to those fledgling acts that would need some advice. I met a lot of movers and shakers in the industry in my travels and learned from them. To this day, I am still learning and using what I have learned to pen this book.

I consider myself very fortunate indeed to have experienced what I have in my years from a teen to today. It is because of this experience that I am able to share with you these events and history. YES, history! Why, because it will never happen again. Music continues to evolve daily and new and exciting performers, bands and sounds will be a part of our daily lives for years to come.

This book will chronicle the life and times of the music in and around the Lehigh Valley area from the 60's to the 90's.

To those of you that were a part of this history, I thank you, and hope you continue to make your contributions to it. AC/ DC said it best "for those about to rock, we salute you".

 INTRODUCTION

For many years people in the Lehigh Valley have been listening to Rock & Roll music and not knowing where it originated from. Truthfully, it wasn't just a sudden thing. It came from the combination of various styles and cultures. Through years of development, we now have a defined sound that is known as Rock & Roll. Some roots and influences of this sound are such genres as bluegrass, blues, rhythm, boogie-woogie, gospel, jazz and rockabilly.

People had new many freedoms and ideas in their heads. Now people were free to pursue individual interests while being guilt free. The music that people wrote and played reflected what was happening around them in society during this time frame.

The Lehigh Valley was no different from the rest of the country. This area has always been a hotbed of music from the early days of Orchestras and Symphonies to the boogie-woogie years of the Great War and later the era of Rock & Roll.

Rock & Roll began to gather steam in the Lehigh Valley in 1956 when area radio stations like WHOL, WEEX, WAEB, WKAP and WSAN began to play the hits of the day. AM stations ruled the airways and the air-personalities, known as Disc-Jockeys began to inject their distinct personalities along with the music to create a sound unique to themselves and their radio stations. Alan Freed was one of the most influential and memorable of these DJ's.

The first R&R song to achieve national acclaim was "Rock Around The Clock "by Bill Haley and The Comets in 1955. Haley succeeded in creating a music that appeared to youth because of its exciting back beat, its call to dance, and the lyrics which for the time were suggestive. The melodies were created by electric guitars and the lyrics were just plain simple. Haley's song ended the era of music that was bland and sentimental that was prevalent in the 40's and early 50's. Haley also succeeded in translating R&B into a sound that adolescent white rock and rollers could relate to. The lyrics articulated the society of the day to include teenage problems, school, cars, summer vacation, parents and the most important things to the kids, young love.

The primary instruments of early rock & roll were guitar, bass, drums and saxophone. All aspects of the music – its heavy beat, loudness, self-absorbed lyrics and raving delivery – indicated a teen defiance of adult values and authority. Some of the performers who influenced the music were Chuck Berry (Johnny B Good), Little Richard (Good Golly Miss Molly), Sam Cooke (You Send Me), Buddy Holly (Peggy Sue), Jerry Lee Lewis (Great Balls Of Fire) and Carl Perkins (Blue Suede Shoes).

The most creative exponent of rock n roll from 1956 – 1963 was Elvis Presley, a truck driver and aspiring singer from Tupelo, MS whose dynamic delivery and uninhibited sexuality appealed directly to young audiences while horrifying the older crowd. Elvis set sales records that stood for years.

At the turn of the decade, Detroit became an important center for black singers. A new sound, known as "The Motown Sound" or "Motor City Sound" developed from this mixture of R&B. It is characterized by a lead singer singing his impressionistic melody story line to the accompaniment of elegant, tight, articulate harmonies or a backup group. Bands who were popular with this style are The Temptations, Smokey Robinson and The Miracles, Diana Ross and The Supremes and Gladys Knight and The Pips.

Rock & Roll was identified by its pulsating drums, repetitive chords, stepped-up tempos and loud guitars. Rock & Roll became the new fad and was well liked by the younger set in the late 50's and early 60's. It gave them a reason to dance and go crazy. It led the way to new clothes and hairstyles among this group. It also led to individuality and the music began to evolve around regional cultures.

One of these legions was made up of mainly mostly teenage male surfers who had an effect on the music. Surfers usually listened to music that originated from Dick Dale and his Del-Tones. Dale released a few songs on his own label and he worked very closely with Leo Fender to improve the Showman guitar and develop the reverberation unit that would give surf music its distinctively fuzzy sound. By the end of 1963, surf music was widely popular. The Beach Boys evolved from this area of music.

By the mid 60's, a new sound was being formed by a number of young bands. It was simple, raw, and crude. Garage bands were usually young and amateur and never really lived up to their inspirations. A lot of these bands actually emphasized their amateurishness by playing the same three chords over and over while at the same time growling their vocals into their microphones. Some say that this was the beginning of do-it-yourself punk rock. Thousands of garage bands popped up in the US and England and the Lehigh Valley was not any different.

The term "Garage Rock" comes from the perception that many such performers were young and amateurish and often rehearsed in the family garage or the garage of a friend. Some of these bands were made up of middle-class teens from the suburbs, rural or urban areas, while some were composed of professional musicians in their 20's & 30's.

The performances were often amateurish or naïve, with typical themes revolving around the traumas of high school life and songs about "lying girls" being particularly common. The lyrics and delivery were notably more aggressive than was common at the time, often with growled or shouted vocals that dissolved into incoherent screaming. Instrumentation was often characterized by the use of guitars distorted through a fuzz box. Nevertheless, garage rock acts were diverse in both musical ability and in style, ranging from crude one-chord music to near-studio musician quality.

While local sock hops, high schools, colleges and clubs catered to this new sound, the teen crowd was drawn to it as " their music ". This was the music of their generation, the baby –boomers. There were many different genres of music to choose from in this era, Rock-A-Billy, Doo Wop, R&B, Soul, Blues, and Jazz all found a happy medium in which to blend their individual influ-

4

ences into new innovative sounds. New styles of music began to rise from this creativity. Top 40 was king and it showed up as the mainstream sounds of the day. There was also the British Invasion, The Underground Sound, Beach Music, Bubble Gum, TV Groups, Hard Rock, the Mersey Beat. A lot of regional sounds such as The Sound of Philadelphia, The Motown Sound, The West Coast Sound, The San Francisco Sound, The Seattle Sound and other that pervaded the music industry in the 60's.

Rock music again surged in popularity with the emergence of The Beatles, a group of long-haired lads from Liverpool, England. They were initially acclaimed for their energy and appealing individual personalities rather than their innovations in their music, which was derived from Chuck Berry and Elvis Presley. Their popularity produced other groups with unusual names. The most popular of these was The Rolling Stones, whose music was derived from the black blues tradition.

Photo by Mark Smith

These British bands instigated a return to the blues orientation of rock & roll, albeit in even louder and more electric and artificial reincarnations.

An important transformation in rock music occurred in 1965 at The Newport Folk Festival when Bob Dylan, noted as a composer of poetic folk and songs of social protest like " Blowing' In The Wind " appeared playing electric guitar and backed by a band with electric instrumentation. A synthesis of the folk revival and rock took place with folk groups using rock arrangements and rock singers composing poetic folk-like lyrics for their songs. Examples of this are The Beatles "Norwegian Wood "& "Eleanor Rigby ". The Byrd's arrangement of Dylan's "Mr. Tambourine Man"is a folk-rock classic. Also performers like The Mamas & Papas, Peter, Paul & Mary, Donavon and The Lovin Spoonful performed music that was now classified as folk-rock.

In the 1960s music mirrored the tensions of the Vietnam War era and played an important role in American culture. The verbal content of rock songs turned toward rebellion, social protest, sex, and, increasingly, drugs. Many groups, among them Jefferson Airplane and Jerry Garcia with the Grateful Dead, tried to approximate in music the aural experience of psychedelic drugs, producing long, repetitive, occasionally exquisite songs with surreal lyrics (known as "acid rock" or "hard rock").

Other groups such as The Strawberry Alarm Clock, Tommy James & The Shondells, The Byrds, Cream, Steppenwolf, Blind Faith and Eric Burdon & the Animals also performed music that was in line with the events and cultures of the day.

In 1967 the Beatles again made history with their album *Sgt. Pepper's Lonely Hearts Club Band*, which, in addition to including drug-oriented songs, presented a body of interrelated pieces that constituted an organic whole. This is considered the first "concept album."

By the late 1960s rock was widely regarded as an important musical form. Musicians such as Miles Davis and John McLaughlin and groups like Traffic or Blood, Sweat, and Tears tried to fuse rock and jazz, while such disparate artists as Leonard Bernstein and Frank Zappa attempted to connect rock and classical music. Groups featuring virtuoso guitarists such as Jimi Hendrix, Eric Clapton, Duane Allman, and Jimmy Page continued to perform variations on classic blues themes using the traditional instruments of rock 'n' roll.

A turning point in rock music occurred in the mid 70's in the form of punk rock, which was a response to the stagnation of the genre and a political statement. Punk was filled with contempt for previous styles of music; its fast-tempoed songs, usually driven by an electric guitar, featured irreverent lyrics often obscured by the clangorous music. British bands such as the Sex Pistols and the Clash quickly became popular in the US and their counterparts here such as The Ramones joined in the fray. By the early 1980's, rock music had changed considerably as groups like Black Flag, the Dead Kennedys and others adopted political protest themes as the core of their music.

In the mid to late 80's, several bands including Nirvana and Pearl Jam continued to follow the path of the early punk rockers by focusing on political themes and celebrating their own lack of technical virtuosity. Punk persisted into the 90's with bands like Green Day and the Offspring. Also in the 90's, was the continuing popularity of the older rock acts, such as the Grateful Dead and the Rolling Stones, bore witness to the enduring appeal of this form among both the young and increasingly middle-aged baby boomers. The appeal of older and past rock bands was also evident in the fanfare surrounding the opening of the Rock and Roll Hall of Fame in Cleveland, Ohio.

CHAPTER ONE: THE GARAGE BAND ERA

During this entire era, clubs were the focal point for bands to get exposure to the masses. Small local clubs sprang up everywhere and it gave these Garage Bands a venue for their music. High schools, colleges and free outdoor concerts were also the rage during these days. Sock Hops, turned into club gigs, which turned into high school and college gigs and then to concerts for those who were fortunate to persevere and go all the way.

Lots of bands produced their own music and recorded it via the promo 45 and sent it to various area radio stations hoping that one of the DJ's or the Music Director would like it and give them airplay. During this era, Payola and Plugola was part of the price a band would have to pay to get promotion of a song or album on the air. Usually this occurred by the Promo Person paying the Radio Person, Program Director or Music Director X amount of dollars for airplay. This practice was exposed and was eventually stopped or went underground.

Radio was the only medium for bands to get exposure for their product, so the best way was for a band to take a demo to a record company hoping to get a contract or to an independent for distribution. These promo copies were then sent to radio stations for the Music Directors to play. The bible for these MD's was R&R (Radio & Records), The Monday Morning Quarterback or Billboard magazine. These were national publications and once your record was listed in it, a radio station would give it a play. A number of stations would let their audiences rate a record and would then make judgments based on that. A lot of bands succeeded in scoring hits this way.

Another area for exposure was local clubs. Club owners would hire bands sometimes to play for the door to see if they would be a draw, or they would be put on a bill with other established bands as openers for the main acts. This was usually the do–or-die for a band. Bands would print their own flyers and plaster them on car windshields, telephone polls, record shops and any other place they could get the word out. Bands that had members from other established bands that had broken up had an advantage on these new guys due to their following they had already established. It was not unusual to see members in 5 different bands in a 5 -6 year period.

Band members also had to purchase their own instruments and many had day gigs to pay for this overhead. At night, they would practice in one of the member's garages to perfect their sound. Hence, the name Garage Bands came into being. It is safe to say at least 90% of the bands from this era had practiced in a garage at one time or another. Why, FREE RENT! Band budgets were all the rage back then. You had to budget for instruments, outfits, flyers, posters and the major costs of a PA system and recording a demo. In those days, when you played for the door at a club, you were lucky to make a hundred dollars, and that was a lot of money then!

In the Lehigh Valley, I was fortunate to hear some of the best Garage Bands ever. Some of these bands made it, some didn't. Some made records, others made memories. There were some local individual performers who made it to the big time and others who are still playing locally today. These are the true dedicated songwriters, composers, lyricists and performers who persevered and have the true love for their music. Listed below are some of the bands from the Garage Band Era in the 60's and early 70's from the Lehigh Valley area that I have had the pleasure of seeing and enjoying their sound.

The Magnificent Men, The Dooley Invention, Frantic Freddie & The Reflections, Uproar, The Combinations, Johnny & The High Keys, The Limits, Dusty Rose, The Kings Ransom, The Union Of Sound, Jay and The Techniques, Kal's Kids/Young Ideas, The Rhythm Machine, The Shillings, The Cyrkle, Steppin Out, The Jordan Brothers, The Misfits, Queens Way Mersey, Slim Pickins, Lord's Estate, Requiem, Wight Reign, Reign Of Iron, The Goodman Brothers, The Graveyard Skiffle Band, Home Brew, Bleu Grass, The Shimersville Sheiks, the NuTones, Rising Tydes, Marigold Circus, Big City Music Band, Andy Starr & The Casinos, Steve Brosky, Cheryl Dilcher, The Columns and RMI-TMI.

The Magnificent Men

The Magnificent Men were also a staple to the Lehigh Valley area. They played a few local clubs and also Notre Dame Bandstand twice with WAEB DJ Gene Kaye. They were mainly into playing bigger venues after their 2nd album hit it big, but made a few appearances at Tom Makoul's Mad Hatter club on Lehigh ST. The Magnificent Men were the first white group invited to play at The Apollo Theater in New York City. The Group also played on bills with some of the top R&B bands of the day including The Four Tops, The O' Jays and The Impressions.

The Magnificent Men were the first white group to ever play the Apollo Theater in New York.

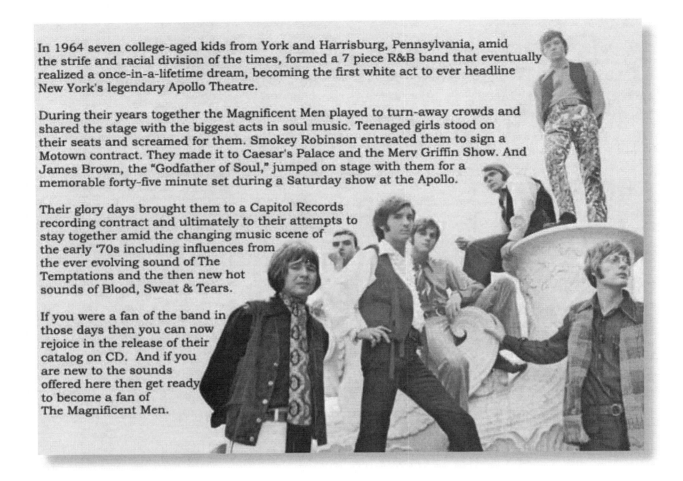

In 1964 seven college-aged kids from York and Harrisburg, Pennsylvania, amid the strife and racial division of the times, formed a 7 piece R&B band that eventually realized a once-in-a-lifetime dream, becoming the first white act to ever headline New York's legendary Apollo Theatre.

During their years together the Magnificent Men played to turn-away crowds and shared the stage with the biggest acts in soul music. Teenaged girls stood on their seats and screamed for them. Smokey Robinson entreated them to sign a Motown contract. They made it to Caesar's Palace and the Merv Griffin Show. And James Brown, the "Godfather of Soul," jumped on stage with them for a memorable forty-five minute set during a Saturday show at the Apollo.

Their glory days brought them to a Capitol Records recording contract and ultimately to their attempts to stay together amid the changing music scene of the early '70s including influences from the ever evolving sound of The Temptations and the then new hot sounds of Blood, Sweat & Tears.

If you were a fan of the band in those days then you can now rejoice in the release of their catalog on CD. And if you are new to the sounds offered here then get ready to become a fan of The Magnificent Men.

FRANTIC FREDDIE AND THE REFLECTIONS

Frantic Freddie Milander was the front man for the Reflections. He helped pen most of the songs on their LP including "You Told a Lie" which was their only hit. Freddie was also a local radio DJ and promoter.

Rare psych-soul local press LP from Easton, PA act circa 1967. This is one of the better musical efforts to come out of the area since the Dorsey brothers. Released by Rice Communications Incorporated, this classic LP has 11 tracks.

1. Hold on to my love
2. My Girl
3. Knock On Wood
4. Someday
5. It Hurts
6. In the Midnight Hour

7. A Day In The Life Of A Teenager
8. Love Em and Leave Em
9. You Told A Lie
10. Sea of Love
11. Why Can't They Understand?
12. You Told a Lie (their big hit)

"FRANTIC FREDDIE," aka Freddie Milander from Coplay, PA recorded this in 1962 with the band, The Proteens which were precursors to Kal's Kids. The B Side is "Love 'Em and Leave 'Em ".

THE DOOLEY INVENTION

The Dooley Invention, an Allentown group who recorded some original songs by the Shillings songwriting team of Jennings & Ross was managed by Dale Schneck. Group members were: Steve Molchany (vocals), Amo Borsetti (organ), Dave Wagner (bass), Wayne Achey (drums) and Richie Kerecz (lead guitar). The Dooley Invention played such venues as King Arthur's Court, The Purple Owl, The Cameo, Odysseus and The Mod Mill. Dooley Invention played and practiced at Illicks Mill. They were known as the area's first band to do an all-original format. Dooley opened for Leslie West and Mountain at the Mad Hatter. Richie Kerch and Steve Mulching eventually moved on to form the band Christian.

THE DOOLEY INVENTION

The Dooley Invention Victorious in 'Battle'

THE DOOLEY INVENTION

After less than a year together, the five members of the Dooley Invention combo captured first place in Monday's "Battle of Bands" contest sponsored by the Whitehall Jaycees.

From here, the boys will enter the state battle in Norristown; if they win that one, it's on to national competition in Massachusetts. At each level, winning combos are in the limelight and there are cash awards and possibilities of recording talent scouts and contracts.

Though the Dooley Invention has played at several teen-age discotheques and dances, it calls the Mod Mill home base. In the beginning, said the leader Rog Stever, they played all types of music; now its strictly folk-rock and "songs with some beauty to them," he said.

Although it is always difficult to compare combos, Rog said his group sounds somewhat like the BeeGees. "But we don't have an organ—and we sound great without it," he said. "I think organs belong in church. Without it we get a much cleaner sound."

The combo includes two Liberty High students, Steve Molchang, vocal, and Wayne Achey, drums; Ritchie Kerec, Freedom, rhythm guitar, and Dave Wagner, Catasauqua, base guitar. Rog, who plays lead guitar, is attending Moravian College Evening Division.

Placing second in the contest were the Columns; the Whispering Campaign placed third.

YOUR GOOD TIMES

The Dooley Invention Logo

The Dooley Invention played at The Roxy Theater in Northampton, PA opening for national act "Fanny". They also worked with Rock and Roll Hall of Fame producer Jeff Barrett who was inducted in 2009.

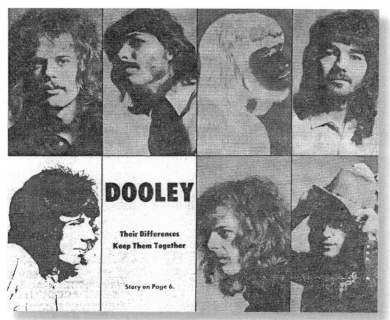

The Dooley Invention or just Dooley as their friends called them

The Dooley Characters: Steve Valek, Dave Wagner, Wayne Achey, Steve Molchany, Arno Borsetti and Dave Smith.

Dooley: Their Differences Keep Them Together

By MARY KOHN
Assistant Teen Times Editor

Dooley: six very serious musicians trying to prove something to the Lehigh Valley. For the past year they have been introducing their listeners to original material.

Many local bands feel that unless they perform popular, commercial music, they will lose their audience. Dooley's vocalist Steve Molchany disagrees. "You're exposing your personality in original material. It's a more personal thing," he said.

It's satisfaction that holds Molchany, Steve Valek, Wayne Achey, Dave Smith, Dave Wagner and Arno Borsetti together. They have confidence in each other and in themselves and fortunately, they haven't reached

the stage some musicians do — overconfidence.

The Dooley Invention was formed in 1968, which makes it one of the most stable bands in the area. They dropped "Invention" after a year or so — nobody ever remembered it anyway, they said. Some members say eventually they will change the name completely.

Dooley is not removed from the people. They really enjoy getting people to "rock out." However, Dooley members don't expect everyone to have to like what they do. "If people don't like what we're doing, we shouldn't get upset about it. No

one will like everything we do because people's tastes are so varied," Molchany said.

Versatility is an important facet of the band. Because each member has a different musical background, it is sometimes difficult to imagine how they could blend together so well. But all of them have been exposed to at least some music theory.

Dave Smith, guitarist, sax, flute and clarinet, is a perfect example of what Molchany means when he says, "A good musician is one who can take theory and put it into something that has real feeling."

Dooley's style runs from folk to beautiful ballads. They can produce everything from intricate jazz numbers to things that the "hogs" will like.

When it comes to having a good jam, Dooley comes with strange things ranging from something that should have been the soundtrack to "2001" to a

medley of standard soul. Sometimes Valek and Molchany (known as the Steve & Steve Show) will top off an entire Firesign Theater routine.

You can often hear Dooley at King Arthur's Court (they're playing there tonight) or jamming at Rick's Mill or Liberty Grange in Bethlehem. On Monday, they'll join other bands in a concert on the SS Amsterdam in New York Harbor.

As with any band, Dooley's days are spent mostly with music. But there was time for everyone but Valek to take up karate last year or for Dave Smith to perfect his horror imitations. And Steve Molchany always has time to trim the locks of the rest of the band.

Three of the members are cycle freaks — not the Hell's Angel kind — but enthusiastic about good bikes.

Dooley has taken it slow and steady since 1968, and though they are looking forward to record contracts someday, they feel rushing it might only ruin it. Meanwhile, they'll keep mak-

ing improvements and changes, and most important, they'll keep enjoying what they do almost as much as their fans.

Dooley Invention article in the Teen Times

14

UPROAR

Here's an early shot of Uproar. Keep in mind, the group spanned 15 years with many members and even toured the states out to California.

In this photo: 1968, Tommy Zito (photos), Janice Barlow Schroth, Kenny Schroth, Arthur Chadwick, Uproar, Gary Gosztonyi, Bob Cirrocco

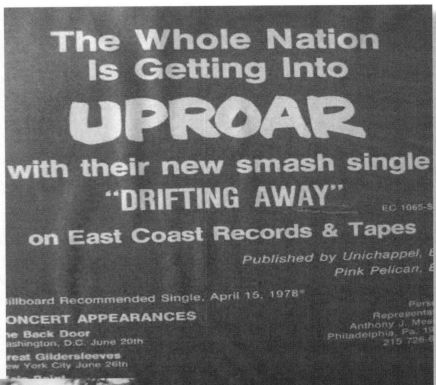

The Whole Nation
Is Getting Into
UPROAR
with their new smash single
"DRIFTING AWAY"
EC 1065-S
on East Coast Records & Tapes
Published by Unichappel,
Pink Pelican,

illboard Recommended Single, April 15, 1978*
ONCERT APPEARANCES
he Back Door
ashington, D.C. June 20th
reat Gildersleeves
ew York City June 26th

Pers
Representa
Anthony J. Mea
Philadelphia, Pa. 19
215 726-6

Lenni, Rick Hamilton, Tommy Zito, Jon Cline, Kenny

THE COMBINATIONS

The Combinations were one of the more successful 60's rock & roll bands to emanate from Pennsylvania. A white band with a black singer, they were welcome in many different diverse locales. Bobby Scammel once said that they could be likened to a Paul Revere & the Raiders if they had been fronted by singer Jackie Wilson. This mix gave birth to an eclectic song set list. They did have a regional hit "Bump Ball "which had a national-tie-in to the popular Milton Bradley game from the 60's.

Left to Right: Marty Freifeld, Bobby Scammell, Sammy Losagio, George Ross and Neil Wellen

The single "Bump Ball" and the Milton Bradley Game

JOHNNY AND THE HIGH KEYS

Johnny & the High Keys were Johnny DeFrancesca (Hammond Organ), Joey Calarusso (Rhythm Guitar & Vocals), Rick Carhart (Bass), Gino Schimpf (Drums), Marty Druckman (Lead Guitar)

The High Keys were local favorites at the clubs of their day and were regulars at King Arthur's Court. Their sound was a mix of blues and rock and roll. I can remember their cover of Three Dog Nights "Try A Little Tenderness" which had Johnny Dee on his Hammond Organ doing a solo that was awesome. Joey Calarusso was a presence as their front man and had a range not often seen in vocalists of the day.

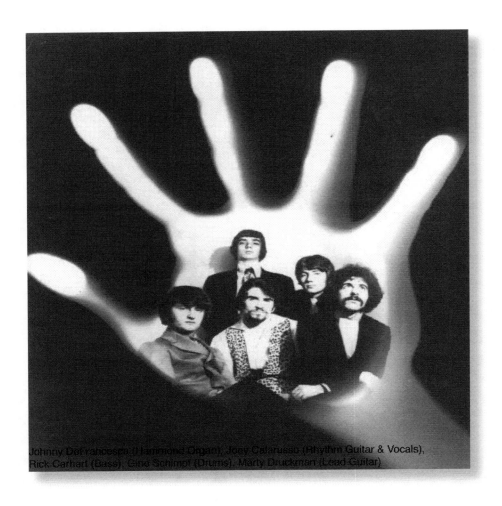

Johnny DeFrancesca (Hammond Organ), Joey Calarusso (Rhythm Guitar & Vocals), Rick Carhart (Bass), Gino Schimpf (Drums), Marty Druckman (Lead Guitar)

JOE COLARUSSO

Their one claim to fame was "THE CHRISTMAS GAME" released on KHP RECORDS in NOV. 1969. That was the closest they came to having a hit record

THE LIMITS

The Limits, one of Eastern Pennsylvania's first Garage/Brit influenced bands, sprang up in Allentown in late 1964. Influenced by The Beatles, Rolling Stones, Kinks, Hollies as well as the soul and R&B groups of the day, they would play raw, passionate songs that showed their love for pop, R&B, as well as Garage and Party Rock. The Limits were one of the busiest local bands, playing teen clubs, high school dances, swim parties, and many hops and promotional events hosted by AM Radio stations WAEB and WKAP.

An Early shot of The Limits from 1965

The Limits in 1966 in Philadelphia

Rick—sporting a beat' look with a pullover and white jeans
'Rook' (Richard) Jones -- quite the Mod guy!
'Beau' (John) Jones -- the 'elder' guy in the band back then (18) playing the upright bass. Quite the nerdy look too!
Chris Jones - co-founder of the band and, although only 14 here, he looks about...11!
Jack Shaffer - a great guy who moved on into The Shillings.

Later drummers for The Limits were Ned Earley (below) & Hub Willson (who played for the Shillings)
Pat McGinley - guitarist, but he also had a great tenor voice. Bruce Ehmer (where'd he get that wig!!) - Bass guitarist, but only briefly

In 1980, after a decade long hiatus, Rick Levy and Beau Jones, a rebirth of The Limits, adding ex-Shillings drummer, Hub Willson, and guitarist, producer, Pete Smoyer. Various sidemen played with the Limits during this time. The band started Luxury Records, and recorded numerous albums and several singles. They also made promotional videos some of which were aired in the early days of MTV and USA Nightflite. They licensed recordings to labels in France and the UK, and performed not only in the Lehigh Valley, but Philadelphia and New York City as well. A compilation CD of their best vinyl entitled "SONGS ABOUT GIRLS" was licensed to Los Angeles based Cleopatra Records in 2010.

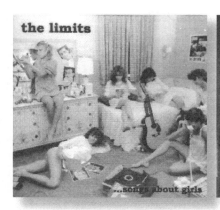

Their early teen recordings have been compiled in a CD, and licensed to Los Angeles based Cleopatra Records. The collection "GARAGE NUGGETS 65-68" contains live, rehearsal, studio covers and originals. The Limits "Close Enough for Government Work" was released in 1985.

The Limits 1966. In this photo: Irwin Goldberg (photos), Ned Earley, Rick Levy, Beau Jones, Christopher Jones. Photo from the Wm. Allen Comus Yearbook

The Limits back in the day at one of their first gigs

The Limits - VOX Battle of the Bands @ the Allentown Fairgrounds in 1967

The Limits drum set from the 1960's

Clockwise from top Chris, Beau, Rook & Rick

The Limits EP – 1985

KING'S RANSOM

King's Ransom started in 1965 in the basement of a friend's house as a band on teenagers with a dream to make it to the big time. Although only about 15-16 at the time, The Kings Ransom with their Rolling Stones influence of bluesy-rock put together their first single " Shame " and " Here Today, Gone Tomorrow ". Their sounds included Bob Werley on his 12-string through a VOX Super Beetle kicking up the mid-range to bring out the sounds emulating The Stones. Before this 45 was released they recorded three songs at the Greek Orthodox Church in Bethlehem. Their manager, Mike Homick, had the songs pressed on one side of 12 inch acetate at Allentown Record Co. The acetates were sent around to various record labels, but remained forgotten and unreleased until recently. Their songs were produced for recording by Pete Helfrich and were released on the newly organized Integra label thru Joe McClaine and Bob Kratz. The band played local clubs like The Mad Hatter, Mod Mill, King Arthur's Court and The Purple Owl.

Bob Dougherty (lead vocals), Vince Homick (rhythm guitar), Bob Werley (lead guitar), Glen Zoski (bass) and Chuck Hoey (drums)

King's Ransom Single

King's Ransom Bumper Sticker

25

Vince Homick

Chuck Hoey

Bob Werley

UNION OF SOUND

During the Mid 60's, The Union of Sound was a big part of the thriving Garage Bands Scene here in the Lehigh Valley. They began their tenure as a clean-cut act but then became to be rowdier bands in the Lehigh Valley. During their reign as a band, they worked steadily at local clubs for the next few years. They befriended local WAEB DJ Gene Kaye and became his house band. They played a lots of frat parties at Lehigh and Lafayette Colleges. The band once backed up The Crystals at the Notre Dame Bandstand. Sadly, their on-stage antics, womanizing and instrument destruction led to their demise. The Union of Sound had no recordings and only a few pictures remain today! The Union of Sound is Tom LaBarge - Guitars & Vocals, Kurt Myers - Guitar & Vocals, Isaac George – Guitar, Jim Higgins – Drums, Craig LaBarge – Bass & Vocals.

Union of Sound at Carroll Hall - CCHS   King Arthur's Court Ad

BIG CITY MUSIC BAND

Big City Music Band was one of the few horn bands in the area at the time and used to play the sounds of Chicago, Blood, Sweat & Tears, Ides of March and other brass oriented sounds. They had a great local following and played almost every local club in the region. They were regulars at King Arthur's Court.

Back Row; Tommy Sestak (drums),Bill Pusey(trumpet/timbales),
Bobby Scammell (Bass/Vocals), Dave Kenney(Sax/Keys/vocals),
Front Row: Fred Bond - RIP(Sax/Vocals),George Berg (Keys/Vocals),
Joe Ziegenfuss (Trombone/Vocals), Steve Mamay (Lead Guitar)

Big City Music Band at the Harrisburg Rock Festival in 1972

JAY & THE TECHNIQUES

Jay & the Techniques was an inter-racial pop group which was formed in Allentown, Pennsylvania during the mid 1960s. A group whose sound and songs were more pop than soul, Jay & the Techniques earned some points for the playful, joyous "Apples, Peaches, Pumpkin Pie," which was their lone Top 10 R&B and pop hit in 1967. Jay and the Techniques still perform today.

"Apples, Peaches, Pumpkin Pie" (1967) - U.S. Pop #6; R&B #8

"Keep The Ball Rolling" (1967) - U.S. Pop #14

"Baby Make Your Own Sweet Music" (1968) - U.S Pop #64

"Strawberry Shortcake (1968) - U.S. Pop #39

"I Feel Love Comin' On" (1974) - U.S. Disco #6

Jay Proctor: Lead vocalist and primary founder of the group , George "Lucky" Lloyd: Second vocalist, Dante Dancho: Lead guitar, Chuck Crowl: Bass guitar, Karl Landis (Lippowitsch): Drums (was replaced by Paul Coles, Jr.), Ronnie Goosley: Saxophone, Jon Walsh: Trumpet (was replaced by Danny Altieri)

Jay & the Techniques on Ed Hurst's Steel Pier Show live from Atlantic City, NJ.

In 1985, Jay Proctor, following a reunion show for "Hands across America", decided to put Jay & The Techniques back together. Rick Levy came on board as manager/guitarist, and since the mid 80s, the group has performed nationally and internationally with a dynamic show of Jay's hits and a classic American soul tribute. Mercury Records in the USA and RPM Records in England have both released Jay & the Techniques' "Best of" collections, and Jay Proctor continues to record as a solo artist for Forevermore Records in Rochester, NY.

THE CYRKLE

The Cyrkle originally was formed by a bunch of Lafayette college students as a frat-rock band in 1966. Before being known as The Cyrkle, their name was The Rhondells. Members of the band were Tom Dawes on bass, guitar & vocals, Don Danneman on guitar, bass & vocals, Earl Pickins on keyboards & vocals and Marty Fried on drums.& vocals. They were influenced by The Four Seasons, Beach Boys and The Beatles and came up with a four-part harmony that was unique for the time. They were first produced by Jerry Ross & DJ Gene Kaye, but that partnership went nowhere fast. After a while Brian Epstein's American liason heard them and then with Brian Epstein brokered their first real record deal.

The name "The Cyrkle" was thought up by none other than John Lennon, who also worked with Epstein. For a while the band was in a holding pattern while Danneman was in the service and Dawes played bass with a then new group with Paul Simon & Art Garfunkel and that is where he first heard "Red Rubber Ball". The band worked with John Simon and he produced their new music for Columbia. "Red Rubber Ball" co written by Paul Simon with Bruce Woodley of The Seekers went to #2 on Billboard's Top 100 and their follow-up "Turn Down Day "peaked at # 16 on Billboard's Top 100.

The band had some member changes, different producers and their last hit "We had A Good Thing Going" was charted on Billboard's Top 100 and peaked at # 66. Danneman did a commercial for for the first 7-Up UnCola campaign that netted the band $10,000. Dawes wrote the "plop, plop, fizz, fizz" jingle for the Alka-Seltzer song.

THE QUEEN'S WAY MERSEY

Another in a long list of local garage bands, **Queen's Way Mersey** never recorded, but was quite popular locally. Guitarist and vocalist Joey Calarusso used his time in the band as a springboard for bigger and better things. Joey also played with The High Keys and also as a solo performer. He is still active today.

Queen's Way Mersey lasted until 1967 when because of a changing music scene that band broke up.

1960's photo of Queeen's Wasy Mersey

The members were Henry "Needles" Mohry – Bass, Tim Kushmar – Rhythm Guitar, Johnny Roth – Lead Guitar, Jerry Wormkessel – Drums, Larry Hahn – Vocals and Joey Colarusso – Guitar & Vocals.

THE SHILLINGS

Mark Jennings and Tom Ross started the original Shillings group, which included Mark (bass, vocals), Tom (guitar, vocals), Al Michailoff (lead guitar) and Ned Earley (drums). In 1967 the line-up was changed to Tom Ross (lead guitar, vocals), Mark Jennings (bass, vocals), Jeff Davis (organ) and Hub Willson (drums). Their first recording was a cover of "Barbara Ann" in late 1965, which was withdrawn when the Beach Boys released their version shortly after. In 1966, their first record, "Laugh," reached number 5 in the Allentown area. The next single, "Lyin & Tryin," written by Tom Ross, stayed on the charts for five weeks in Allentown, Connecticut and Boston. The Shillings were managed by Dale Schneck who also managed the Dooley Invention, an Allentown group who recorded some original songs by the Shillings songwriting team of Jennings & Ross.

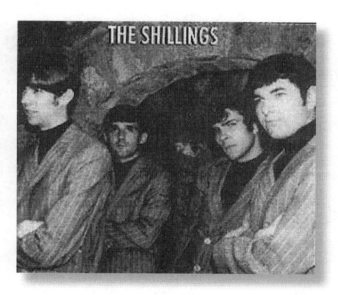

The Allentown, PA, group the Shillings had local hits with "Laugh" and "Lyin' and Tryin'" in the mid-'60s. Both songs are included on this collection, which is largely devoted to original material, although it also has fairly good covers of Jackie DeShannon's "Children and Flowers" and Barry Mann and Cynthia Weil's "You Baby" (done in the '60s by the far more famous acts the Ronettes, the Lovin' Spoonful, and Sonny & Cher). The Shillings were a rather modestly talented group that inhabited the lightest, most pop-oriented area of the '60s garage rock playing field, with vocal harmonies heavily shaded with the likes of the Beatles, the Beau Brummels, and

The Lovin' Spoonful. That doesn't mean that the record isn't enjoyable, though it's not imbued with great innovation or significance. Their songs bounce along with a nice pleasantly melodic innocence, sometimes venturing into a gooier pool, as on the orchestrated "Strawberry Jain." In other tracks, they reflect yet other trends of the day, "Wild Cherry Lane" using a soulful horn section and "Seems Like Yesterday" deploying a cool gloomy Zombies-like organ, while "You Can Show Me the Way" sounds like one of the Monkees' more credible early tracks. As a tentative step into psychedelia, "Crimson Afternoon" is impressive in its melancholy organ-driven haze, though like much of the LP it has only fair sound quality.

THE GOODMAN BROTHERS

After returning from overseas, Billy Goodman hooked up in Pennsylvania with his brother Frank who had been writing songs in Mexico. They already sang like only brothers can and used Frank's original songs and Billy's newfound prowess on the bottleneck guitar to form the Goodman Brothers. This duo went on for a year until they found guitar legend Steve Kimock (Zero, Phil Lesh and Friends) in a local bar, and with their sister Kelley and a few friends started the cult favorite Goodman Brothers Band in Bucks County, Pa.

 Clockwise from top: Frank, Billy Goodman, Duffy Hoffman & Steve Kimock (lower right pic)

The Goodman Brother's - 1968.

Goodman Brothers Promo

The band played their progressive brand of original folk, rock and blues for seven exciting and turbulent years. Despite their popularity, however, they were never signed by a major record label. Perhaps it was due to their mixed style or just the way the music business was developing. In 1982 the band ultimately broke up and Billy sobered   up to a world where the music had changed. Steve Kimock went on to play with artists like Jerry Garcia and a host of others.

35

THE SILHOUETTES

Another version of the Silhouettes (there were many) circa 1972 with Big Daddy Dave (Drums and Vocals), Tom Sines - not pictured (Sax and Vocals), Judy (Rhythm Guitar and Vocals), Dave G (Lead guitar), and Ely Sines (Bass and Vocals)

This picture was taken at the New Orleans Lounge, Allentown, PA. The New Orleans Lounge was known for its R&B bands as well as regional and national acts that were booked there throughout the years and was located in center city Allentown.

ANDY STARR AND THE CASINOS

These guys got their start in the Lehigh Valley. They were from the Bethlehem & Nazareth area. They met and recorded their first 2 songs with Pete Helfrich and were promoted by Gene Kaye.

In later years, they got a connection with casino records and recorded and released "I Know It's True "and "My Love for You ". The next set of music was "Why Am a Fool "By the Casinos and "I Love You Baby "By Andy Starr. These were released on 2 different labels, Casino and Arcade Records. Both records were released on Oct 12, 1959. Both records made the Top 40 in the Lehigh Valley and surrounding areas, but never went national.

THE SCOTT BEDFORD FOUR

The Scott Bedford Four was another of those Lehigh Valley garage bands with aspirations. They took their talents to another level and wrote and recorded at least 4 songs, 4 for the Joy label "You Turned Your back On Me", "Manhattan Angel", "Last Exit To Brooklyn" and "How Does It Feel" and one on the Congress label "You Turned Your back On Me" which was their first on their original label before moving to Joy where they re-mastered the song and re-recorded it.

The Scott Bedford Four have a good commercial mid-'60s rock sound that borrows from soul and the British Invasion, particularly on "You Turned Your Back on Me." Occasionally (as on "Manhattan Angel" and "Last Exit to Brooklyn"), they also draw from the harmonies of the Beach Boys and more mainstream groups like Jay & the Americans to a pleasant effect.

"Last Exit to Brooklyn" has a Vogues feel to it.

DIANE SANDS

Diane Sands, Jay Sands daughter, recorded her 1 hit wonder in the late 60's. Her song got airplay locally in the region, and was supported by her father and received heavy airplay on WAEB, but the song was short lived and she never recorded a follow up to the tune. She performed her tune at area lounges and clubs. She was once married to DJ Johnny Michaels, another WAEB and WSAN local air personality.

Diane Sands "Don't Take Your Love Away" recorded on Reading Records in the late 60's

Diane Sands circa mid-1960's

MARIGOLD CIRCUS

Marigold Circus played the local club scene along with high schools and fire companies. They had an eclectic garage sound that can only be described as different and unusual. They were rockers in the mold of a classic garage band with their raw sound and choice of covers that they performed.

Marigold Circus promo photo circa 1968, Left to right: John Fretz (bass), Steve Vallek (guitar), Terry "McGraw" Palmer (drums) Kenny Siftar

Marigold Circus painted drum head - a lost art!

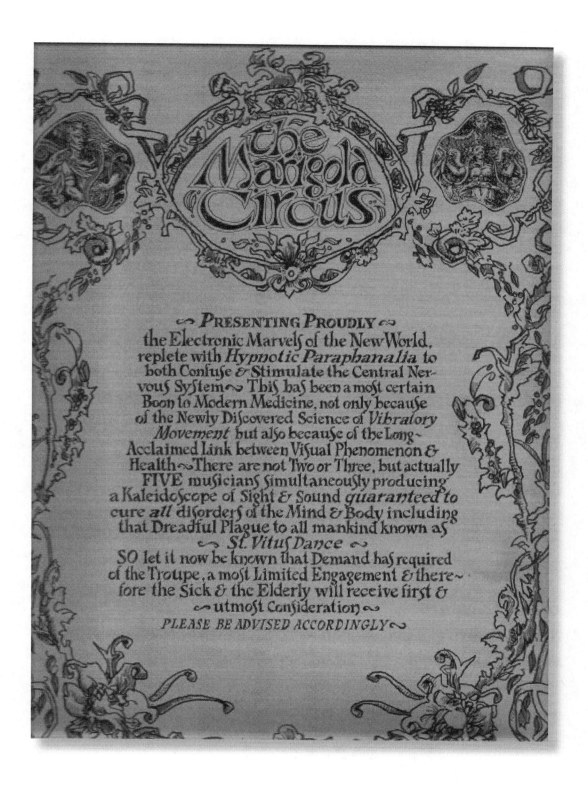

the Marigold Circus

~ PRESENTING PROUDLY ~
the Electronic Marvels of the New World,
replete with *Hypnotic Paraphanalia* to
both Confuse & Stimulate the Central Ner-
vous System ~ This has been a most certain
Boon to Modern Medicine, not only because
of the Newly Discovered Science of *Vibratory
Movement* but also because of the Long~
Acclaimed Link between Visual Phenomenon &
Health ~ There are not Two or Three, but actually
FIVE musicians simultaneously producing
a Kaleidoscope of Sight & Sound *guaranteed to*
cure *all* disorders of the Mind & Body including
that Dreadful Plague to all mankind known as
~ *St. Vitus Dance* ~
SO let it now be known that Demand has required
of the Troupe, a most Limited Engagement & there~
fore the Sick & the Elderly will receive first &
~ utmost Consideration ~
PLEASE BE ADVISED ACCORDINGLY ~

Center Window - Jack Syverchek   Bottom Left Window - Jim Roman, drums
Top Left Window - Bob Reppert, lead guitar   Top Center Window - Mike Pella, bass
Right Window - Steve Valek

44

THE JORDAN BROTHERS

The Jordan Brothers are Joe, Lou, Frank & Bob Jordan.

Jamie Recording Artists, the Jordan Brothers from Frackville, PA. Their first release was "Send Me Your Picture" and their biggest hit "Gimme Some Lovin'" was released in the US before the more successful version by The Spencer Davis Group. The Jordan Brothers toured with Dick Clark's Caravan of Stars bus tour and appeared on numerous Philadelphia and New Jersey-based TV shows. They played numerous times in the Lehigh Valley area.

James Henke, chief curator from The Rock & Roll Hall Of Fame named "Gimme Some Lovin"
by The Jordan Brothers as one of the 500 songs that helped shape Rock & Roll History.

Maxim Furek, a former music critic, also penned The Jordan Brothers: A Musical Biography of
Rock's Fortunate Sons, which detailed the career of Frackville's legendary rock band. Furek's
efforts led to a Jordan Brothers Reunion in 1986 and a special proclamation from the Schuylkill
County Commissioners.

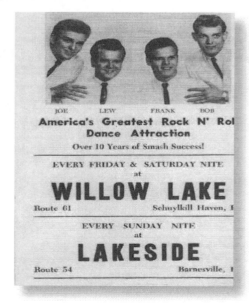

CHRISTIAN

Christian was a rockin band in the Lehigh Valley in the 70's. They played all the local rock clubs and held the Wednesday night attendance record at Bill Daniels Rock Palace. Bill Daniels would always go on stage to introduce the band and that was always a thrill because you never knew what he was going to say.

clockwise from lower left: Jerry Ruttman, Stephen Molchany, Bob Trump, Rich Kerecz, Lou Napoli

STEVE MOLCHANY

Steve Molchany was a rock and roll staple in the Lehigh Valley for many years. From his days playing guitar and doing vocals with Dooley Invention and playing the teen clubs to rocking out with Christian where he wrote and performed many of his original tunes and played the areas hottest clubs to the band Clue where a balanced mixture of covers and originals was their forte to the duet he did with Riche Kerecz, Steve was a consummate musician.

Steve once said "Versatility is an important facet of the band, because each member has a different musical background. It is difficult to imagine how we could blend together so well. We all had exposure to music theory. A good musician is one who can take theory and put it into something that has real feeling".

SLIM PICKINS

Slim Pickins were rockers without boundaries. They formed in 1971 after the breakup of In-Sex. They were a jamming blues-rock band that energized and excited audiences wherever they played. Throughout the years, Pickins played their own brand of rock that often left their audiences numb and mesmerized. If a band could be called the rock rebels, it was Slim Pickins. Their blend of blues, rock and some rock-a-billy gave them a distinctive edge over most of their counterparts of the era. Pat "The Hat "Cush was known for his often off–the-cuff antics on stage and was also very outspoken. Manfred Kodilla was the equalizer in the band and Jack Riskey was the "Wild Child". Paul Buchanan replaced Manfred Kodilla on bass after their Cali adventure. Their classic hit "Out on the Farm", recorded during their Neff's day's, was their big hit. Their music still is talked about today and the masses yearn for a reunion.

Pat Cush, Manfred Kodilla, Jack Riskey... Original Slim
Pickins right after the In-Sex broke up.
(Photo courtesy of Manfred Kodilla)

Pat 'the hat' Cush in the 70's

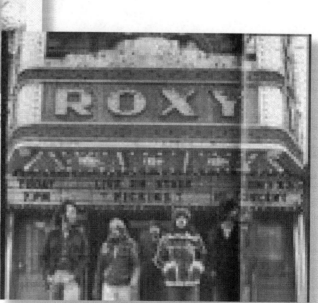

Slim Pickins headlined at The Roxy Theater

Slim Pickins LP "First Time Around"

Slim Pickins 45 "Wham Bam"

THE ADVENTURERS

The Adventurers were from Catasauqua, PA. This 45 rpm single was their only release on the now defunct Reading Record label. The members of the band were Amedeo Borsetti, Jim Smith, Dave Wagner and Denny Wagner.

"Baby, Baby My Heart "and b/w "Baby Doll By "

RMI – TMI

RMI – TMI was another one of those bands that used horns to energize their audience. They were regulars at Illick's Mill in Bethlehem in the early 70's. Their fat sound with their Hammond Organ with Leslie backed by the horn section and dual vocals added harmonies to the bland cover tunes that they performed. They were a crowd favorite at The Mill.

RMI - TMI performing at Illick's Mill, Bethlehem, PA, September 15, 1972. Left to right: Rob Freeman (keyboards), Mike Barbiero (vocals), John Markel (vocals), Paul Jost (drums), Marty Balk (bass), Jared Melson (trombone), Nick Sabatini (sax), Jim "Honk" Avey (sax & flute)
In this photo: Rob Freeman (photos), Mike Barbiero, John Markel, Paul Jost (photos), Martin Balk.

CLUE

NIGHT ON THE TOWN

Professor Clouseau would have no trouble tracking down **Steve Molchany** these days. He'd find a **Clue** almost everywhere he'd look, the most recent one being at Scarlett O'Hara's in Bethlehem, where Molchany and his new group played last weekend.

Clue probably is one of the most polished rock acts to appear in this area. The group, with Bethlehemite Molchany on vocals, also includes **Tony Corona** of Easton on vocals and sax, **Dan Frederick** of Allentown on lead guitar, **Dave Frederick** of Allentown on bass, **Joe Milutis** of Easton on keyboards, and **Craig Coyle** of Bethlehem on drums.

The band had been together as Nightflyte before Steve joined. Clue's sound is tight, but allows each musician to step out as an instrumentalist.

The group is capable of unstrained harmonies, with Corona singing emotive leads on some songs like Bobby Caldwell's "What You Wouldn't Do for Love."

Molchany handles the vocals on material ranging from Billy Joel's "My Life" and "Big Shot" to Barry Manilow's "Copacabana (At The Copa)."

"We're working on original material," Molchany said. "The band's been together for a while. I can't take credit for that. They more or less asked me to join because they wanted to go in the direction of doing their own material.

"They were doing some of their own material when I first checked the band out. But it's kind of tough to do it in a club where people just want to dance."

Molchany, a Liberty High School graduate, first burst on the area rock scene with Dooley Invention, which was together from 1968 to 1972, and,

says Molchany, "had a larger turnover than McDonald's."

There also was Crossfire, Raven, and perhaps most notably, Christian, which he formed with his longtime friend and songwriting partner, Richie Kerecz, who now has his own recording studio in Allentown.

Molchany was sidelined with a back injury (two discs had to be removed) in 1977. He was fronting Dreams until last October when, he jokes, the band "was dashed to the rocks."

Molchany is cognizant of the difficulties any group has in landing a recording contract. "There was a lot more room for experimentation several years ago, but it just seems to have gotten crushed out," he said.

But Molchany, who is performing full-time now, is optimistic about Clue's chances. From the start, things seemed right, he said. After all, the group's first gig was New Year's Eve at the Shawnee Inn in the Poconos.

Area fans can find Clue at Phase V in Bethlehem next Friday.

PAUL A. WILLISTEIN JR.

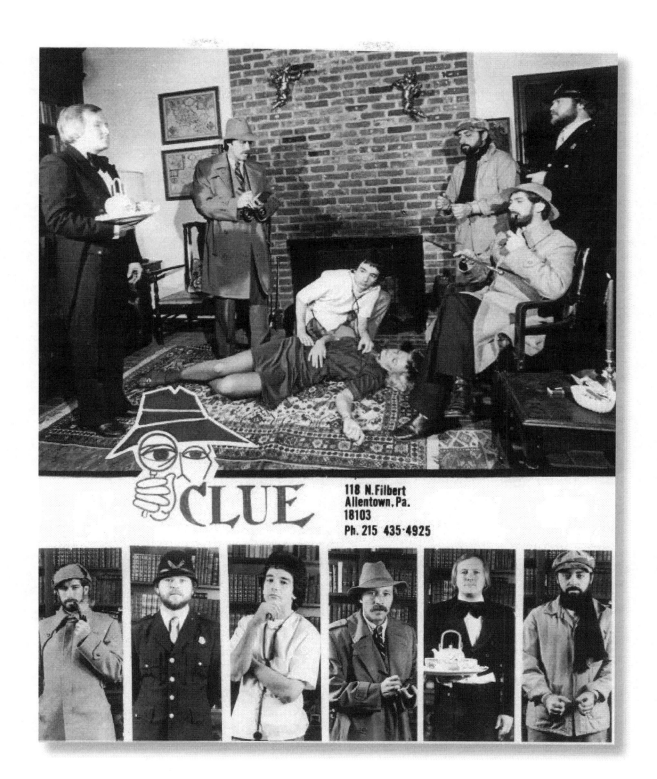

CLUE

118 N. Filbert
Allentown, Pa.
18103
Ph. 215 435·4925

THE COLUMNS

The Columns were a popular club band in the Lehigh Valley area in the mid to late 60's. The band was formed in 1966 by The Frey Brothers and some friends from school. They started off playing school dances, block parties and frat parties and then went into the Lehigh Valley club circuit. At that time, there were a plethora of clubs to play in the area. The played rooms such as The Mod Mill, King Arthur's Court, Third Eye, Jamaican A Go-Go and The Red Beat Lounge.

The Columns: Russ Lichtenwalner (bass guitar), Gary Gritz (lead guitar), Randy Frey (crouching, lead vocals), Brad Frey (drums), Ron Henniger (rhythm guitar) and Steve Rosatti (keyboards). Tom Bluder (vocals) not pictured

Notice the painted Drum Head on the Bass Drum!

CHERYL DILCHER - RIP

Cheryl Dilcher began her musical career in her hometown of Allentown, Pennsylvania. Accompanying herself on the 12-string guitar, she played her self-penned songs at concerts on college campuses in the Lehigh Valley in the late 1960s and early 1970s. Some of the colleges she played include Lafayette College (Easton), Lehigh University (Bethlehem), and Muhlenberg College (Allentown).

In 1967, a self-styled record producer from Red Bank, New Jersey, Johnny Dee (John DeCesare), was looking for a musical act to manage, produce, and record. Johnny wanted to meet with Cheryl on her home turf, so they drove from New Jersey to Allentown, Pennsylvania, to her apartment with a beautiful bay window over a corner luncheonette (401-1/2 Gordon Street). We stayed at a hotel downtown and, because we didn't have much money, we brought along our camping stove and cooler and cooked dinner in the room all three of us shared.

Johnny, in his inimitable fashion, decided to record Cheryl with part of her boyfriend Wayne's band: Wayne Achey on drums; John Adelson on lead guitar, organ, and harmonica; Dave Wagner on bass guitar; and Amedeo Borsetti on electric piano and organ. Lane Emley played bass guitar also. The other players were studio musicians who Johnny hired.

For background vocals, he brought in a young woman who was gigging around the city, picking up studio work to supplement her regular night performing at the Continental Baths--Bette Midler. RIP - Cheryl who was born on November 12, 1946, died on February 26, 2005

Special Songs was released in 1970

Butterfly was released in 1973

Cheryl also released 2 more LP's Magic in 1974 and Blue Sailor in 1977

JOHNNY'S DANCE BAND

Johnny's Dance Band is Johnny Jackson, Chris Darway, Tony Juliano & Paul Messing.

JDB was influenced by the British Invasion and various artists like the Beatles, Young Bloods, Jefferson Airplane, Peter, Paul and Mary, Gordon Lightfoot and Eric Andersen. JDB performed in local coffee houses, teen clubs and local & regional nightclubs from Philly to Reading to The Lehigh Valley. Nan Mancini joined the band in 1974. Early recordings were at Sigma Sound and eventually recorded three albums on the RCA/Wind Song label, and later recorded in NYC at Jimi Hendrix Electric Ladyland Studios.

Original 1968 Lineup

Original Johnny's Dance Band, 1969

1974 band lineup with Nan Mancini

Johnny's Dance Band Logo

DUSTY ROSE

Dusty Rose was made up of experienced musicians from the Lehigh Valley area. They played the local club scene at places like the Queen Victoria.

Dusty Rose is Chris Jones, Denny Danko, Peggy Salvatore, Howard Schneider, Hub Willson, and Joey Hammerl.

PF AND THE FLYERS

In this photo: Craig Coyle, Pete Fluck, Alan Gaumer, Davey Frederick and Mike Krisukas. This was the original band. Pete Fluck, Alan Gaumer and Mike Krisukas are still active performers today.

An original PF and the Flyers T-shirt.

STEPPIN OUT

Steppin Out was a very experienced band. Hub Willson had played with The Shillings and The Limits, Dave Fry was an accomplished songwriter and composer and the talents of the rest of the guys made this band a Valley favorite for many years. The band was known to play outdoor gigs in the summer and made the circuit of the Valley's club outlets back in the day. The band was a favorite at the Queen Victoria.

In this photo: Christopher Jones, Reid Tre, Dave Fry, Jeff Biro, Hub Willson and Dennis Danko

The band played an outdoor gig at Allentown's Union Terrace. In this photo: Chris Jones, Reid Tre, Dave Fry, Dennis Danko and Hub Willson.

Chris Jones, Reid Tre, Dave Fry and Dennis Danko

Chris Jones, Tre Reid, Jeff Biro, Dave Fry, Dennis Danko and Hub Willson

Steppin" Out, back in the day.

Steppin" Out, dressed to kill!

LITTLE TOMMY ZITO

Tommy Zito's career began very early in life. He was a young man when he recorded his first single "I Played a Trick on Santa Claus" which was written by WKAP DJ Les Baer. This holiday song became the favorite of people in the Valley and was played on most of the local radio stations at the time. This was just the beginning of his stellar career which has included Uproar, Magnum, Aviator and The Piano Man, Tommy Zito, as a soloist.

Little Tommy Zito with Max Hess at Hess's Department Store.

Hess's record department store clerk presenting Tommy Zito with the first record received on the Wan-Dell label. "I Played a Trick On Santa Claus" was written in part by local radio personality Les Baer.

D.B.I.L.I.T.Y.

The name D.B.I.L.I.T.Y. stood for "dress British, look Irish, think Yiddish" The band was led by Dave Peifly, who would later go on to play bass for Daddy Licks. The band was formed in 1975. Several weeks after the formation of the band, they went into the studio where they recorded 4 songs, "Go West Young Man", "Life", "33 Years Past" and " Get Down or Get Out". In all, the band recorded 22 songs. The first four tunes launched the band into the local club scene.

They were booked into venues like The Green Pine Inn, The Red Rooster, The Huckster, The Lemon Tree, The Maple Grove, The Queen Victoria and area college frats by Sam Losagio and Dave Sestak from Media V Entertainment. The band was managed by Dave Schneck who had also managed such local acts as The Shillings and Dooley Invention.

D.B.I.L.I.T.Y. was originally a five-man band, but that number was paired down to four, Dave Peifly, Andy Green, Greg McCoy and Terry Gross. Andy Green went on to work with John Cale for 15 years. Dave Peifly owned Play It Again Records (opened in 1980), Toones (purchased in 1984) and Positively 19th Street.

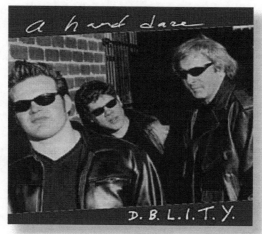

D.B.I.L.I.T.Y. in the 1970's.

SHIMERSVILLE SHEIKS

The **Shimersville Sheiks** were another of those Lehigh Valley bands that was borne from other bands. The members had a lot of experience between them and soon became Valley favorites. They had what can be called a cult following in the area during their tenure. Their mixture of Bluegrass, Country and Folk music was a refreshing diversion from music of the day. The band played venues like The Queen Victoria and Godfrey Daniels as well as folk festivals.

The Shimersville Sheiks are Chris Simmons, Dave Fry, Jerry Bastoni and Dave Smith.

The Shimersville Sheiks at the Muhlenberg College Folk Festival in the 70's.

KAL'S KIDS

Kal's Kids was the brainchild of Kal Kastelnik. Kal was the owner of Kal's Music in Whitehall, PA and sold musical instruments to many Lehigh Valley musicians. Kal was also a music instructor who has taught hundreds of area boys and girls how to play an instrument.

During this period of the early to mid 60's, Kal would put together some of his brightest and talented students in a band setting and this became "Kal's Kids" There were several different versions of Kal's Kids over the years. Some of the members who have played at one time or another in the band include Craig Kastelnik (guitar), Butch Kastelnik-RIP(drums), Alan Gaumer (horns), Rich Picirilli(sax), Blaise DeMicilli(acordian), Tony Fasching-RIP, Billy Fasching and Lenny Martucci.

Kal's Kids appeared with the stars of TV also. Sally Starr, Chief Halftown and Bertie the Bunyip are some of the notables. The band had a big break when they were asked to appear on the CBS show, Ted Mack's Amateur Hour, a half-hour show that was dedicated to bringing new and upcoming acts to the public.

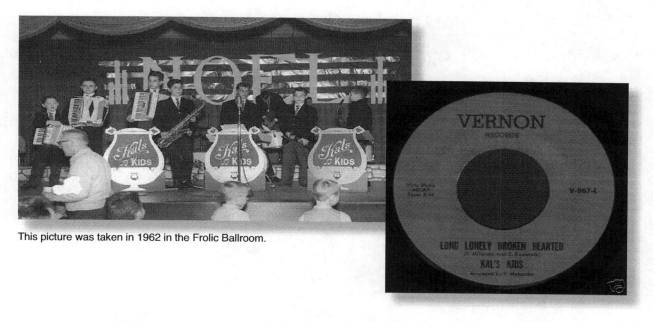

This picture was taken in 1962 in the Frolic Ballroom.

"Long Lonely Broken Hearted "is a killer sweet soul tune written by Frantic Freddie Milander and Craig Kastelnik. The B Side is "Oh Ronnie ". This was recorded at Virtue Recording Studios in Philadelphia. These songs were recorded in the later years of the group.

Several bands that emerged from Kal's Kids included The Proteens, who had a single on White Rock Records "Love Em or Leave Em" and a Lehigh Valley favorite, The Young Ideas.

Sadly Tony Fasching and Butch Kastelnik are deceased but Craig Kastelnik and Alan Gaumer are still active and playing in the Valley today.

THE GRAVEYARD SKIFFLE BAND

The early Graveyard Skiffle Band with Jan Sprague, Chris Simmons, Bob Flower, Dave Fry.

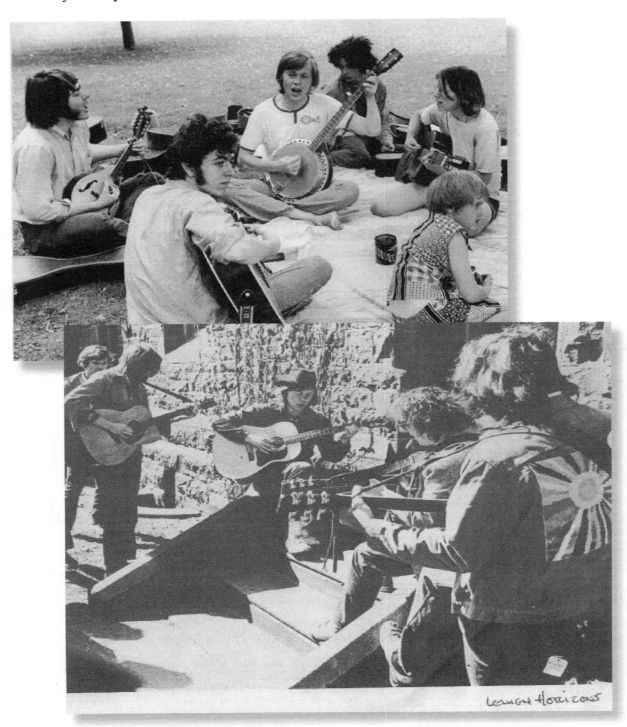

BLINDMAN'S BLUFF

Blindman's Bluff, circa 1971, with Manny Julio, John Seremula, Missing Greg (Muchas) Frey, Bob Stuber, David Pierce. This picture was taken on the other side of Springtown off Funk's Mill Road possibly near the old Haupt's Bridge.

THE MUNCHKINS

The Munchkins were another one of those local garage bands were popular for a few years before the players went their separate ways. Thom Mooney & Craig Bolan were the principles in the band and did most of the arranging and songwriting.

The band played at The Mod Mill, Illicks Mill, and many other Lehigh Valley haunts before disbanding. They had that raw sound which would attract you to them and hold you with their presentation. They were very popular with the teen crowd.

Thom Mooney and Craig Bolan went on to play with Todd Rundgren and The Nazz after the Munchkins broke up.

THE VAGRANTS

The Vagrants prominently featured a Hammond Organ in their music and often played soul-influenced rock. The Vagrants were far more guitar-based than say The Rascals were, but projected a more garage, less mature outlook than other bands of the era.

One of the few bands signed to the folkie Vanguard label, they recorded some singles between 1965 and 1968. After that they were signed to Atco and they did a rock cover of Otis Redding's "Respect" which was a hit in the Northeast and also "I Can't Make a Friend".

The group broke up in 1968 and band member Leslie West went on to form the band Mountain of "Mississippi Queen" fame. The Vagrants played at Bethlehem PA's Illick's Mill.

The Vagrants clockwise from bottom left: Leslie West, Roger Mansour, Jerry Storch, Larry West and Peter Sabatino.

THE SOUND OF TIMES

This band played around the area for a few years and was a regular at Saylor's Lake Pavilion. Driven by the beat of drummer Dan Kocher, the band played the hot tunes of the day and some classic mixed in for good measure.

In this photo: Dan Kocher – Drums, Mike Tiedman – B3 Organ, Kenny Myers Vocals

Saylors Lake Tavern
1966

JAMES BYNAM

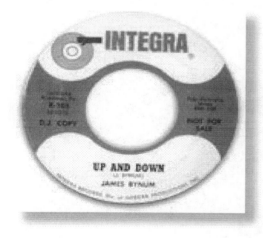

This single is a nice double-sider from Allentown PA that's not going to change your world but it should get you up on your feet and on the floor, this side is a gritty sixties northern dancer while the flip is a bit of an R&B groover that should be well known to some but is a bit of an obscurity around these parts.

James Bynam recorded one of the best 70s dancers on the northern scene "Time Passes By". A 1975 recording from the Philly City label, it contains one of the heaviest bass lines ever put on record.

Bynam was a local Philly guy, who played the Lehigh Valley scene. He's a gospel singer now.

THE UNIQUE TOUCH

Unique Touch did a mixture Top 40, Rock, Funk R&B and some country. Their main influence was The Buddy Rich Band. The band played high schools and fire companies before moving into a short stint in the club scene. They were the epitome of a garage band as they were still in school when this pic was taken.

The Unique Touch with Denny Wagner filling in on Bass is the brother of Dave Wagner from Dooley Invention.

BLEU GRASS

Bleu Grass was a late '60s Allentown group who met at Illick's Mill. Influenced by the under-rated first Mandrake Memorial album, they won the Allentown JCC Battle of the Bands, resulting in a trip to ABE recording studio and a limited edition 45. The band members were John Fretz (bass), Barry Blinderman (vocals), Rob Freeman (RMI rock-si-chord, backing vocals), Bruce Sheftel (drums) and Gregg Smith (guitar). Gregg's younger brother, Mark Smith, founded the Creatures of The Golden Dawn, who still perform music to this day.

What I Know," A-side of Bleu Grass self-produced
45RPM single, 1969

"Strange Haze," B-side of Bleu Grass self-produced
45RPM single, 1969

THE ROYAL DUKES

Dan Kocher age 10, David Shellhammer owner, and the **Royal Dukes** performing at the Royal Palms night club, before it was Bill Daniels Rock Palace and Caesar's Palace.

ALLENTOWN ANGLOPHILE

I cannot say enough about these compilations and the history that goes along with them. Dave Peifly, a local music affectionado, has put together some of the finest songs from the Garage Bands era of the 60's and the rock era from the 70' & 80's on his Allentown Anglophile series of LP's.

Most of what I have featured here in this book are available on these disks. Most of these recordings are very rare and cannot be found elsewhere. You may come across a few at a record collectors show, but that is few and far between.

Dave has compiled music from the Lehigh valley that made the area what is, a hotbed of music and originality. As you sit down and listen to these comps, it takes you back to a simpler time when rock music was evolving into what it is today. Here are the comps of Allentown Anglophile:

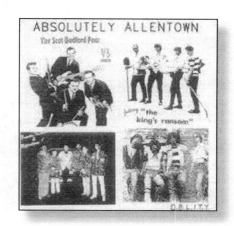

01. SCOTT BEDFORD FOUR - You Turned Your Back On Me (2:23)
02. SCOTT BEDFORD FOUR - Mowin' The Lawn (2:15)
03. SCOTT BEDFORD FOUR - Hey There Girl (1:55)
04. SCOTT BEDFORD FOUR - Manhattan Angel (2:33)
05. SCOTT BEDFORD FOUR - Last Exit To Brooklyn (2:17)
06. JORDAN BROTHERS - Gimme Some Lovin' (2:38)
07. JORDAN BROTHERS - The One That Got Away (2:15)
08. JORDAN BROTHERS - It's A Shame (2:17)
09. JORDAN BROTHERS - Good Times (2:01)
10. KINGS RANSOM - Shadows Of Dawn (2:12)
11. KINGS RANSOM - Mistakes (3:13)
12. KINGS RANSOM - Street Car (2:46)
13. SHILLINGS - Just For You Baby (2:32)
14. SHILLINGS - Strawberry Jain (2:52)
15. RONDELLS - Parking In The Kokomo (2:23)
16. YOUNG IDEAS - Barney Buss (2:20)
17. COMBINATIONS - Bump Ball (2:08)
18. LIMITS - Just Another Girl (3:07)
19. "FRANTIC" FREDDIE MILANDER - Charmaine (2:17)
20. JOHNNY & THE HIGH-KEYS - Do You Believe (2:27)
21. JOHNNY & THE HIGH-KEYS - The Christmas Game (2:27)
22. I, SHE & WE - McDougal Street (2:07)
23. D.B.L.I.T.Y. - Out On The Road (3:06)
24. D.B.L.I.T.Y. - Stay Away From Whiskey (2:28)
25. SLIM PICKINS - Out On The Farm (3:18)
26. DADDY LICKS - She Said No (3:12)
27. DADDY LICKS - South Street Boogaloo (3:59)
28. STEVE BROSKY - Hey Now (Do The Dutch) (3:05)
29. STEVE BROSKY - King Of The Queen Victoria (3:20)
30. ST. JOHNS ALLIANCE - Mark My Words (2:09)

Mastered By: T.Shefenik
More Info: www.allentownanglophile.com
Contact: positively19@hotmail.com

1. BIG CITY MUSIC BAND featuring STEVE KINOCK - Lazy (6:44)
2. COMBINATIONS - Watcha Gonna Do (2:44)
3. COMBINATIONS - Hey! Uncle Sam (2:46)
4. MARIGOLD CIRCUS - Rock Me (4:00)
5. QUEEN'S WAY MERSEY - Hey Gyp (5:06)
6. QUEEN'S WAY MERSEY - Under My Thumb (2:40)
7. HIGH KEYS - It's Alright (3:49)
8. OGNIR AND THE NITE PEOPLE - I Found A New Love (2:01)
9. ANGIE AND THE CITATIONS - Salt And Pepper (2:43)
10. ANGIE AND THE CITATIONS - I Wanna Dance (2:00)
11. DEVILS - The Devil Dance (2:47)
12. DEVILS - Just Like That (2:23)
13. BENTLEYS - Now It's Gone (2:38)
14. MORTICIANS - Now That You've Left Me (2:28)
15. CHOSEN FEW - Staircases, Please And Time (2:49)
16. HI-BOYS - Girls In The Groove (2:57)
17. SCOTT BEDFORD FOUR - How Does It Feel (2:15)
18. KINGS RANSOM - Ain't That Just Like Me (2:55)
19. KINGS RANSOM - Decent Part Of Life (4:27)
20. SHILLINGS - Wild Cherry Lane (2:17)
21. SHILLINGS - Crimson Afternoon (2:35)
22. DOOLEY INVENTION - Who Spent The Night Inside Your Mind (2:17)
23. BLEU GRASS - Strange Haze (3:00)
24. D.B.L.I.T.Y. - Jailbait (2:55)
25. LIMITS - Wipeout (2:45)

Mastered by: T. Shefenik

Other titles available from Positively 19th Street include Scott Bedford Four, Shillings, D.B.L.I.T.Y., Afro Gant, Daddy Licks, King's Ransom, Allentown Anglophile, Absolutely Allentown, Allentown Awlspring

Requests for CD's should be made through Positively 19th Street, 522 N. 19th. St. Allentown Pa. (610)435-4585 Mon-Sat 11-6pm est.
e-mail orders Positively19@hotmail.com
More Info: www.allentownanglophile.com

ABSOLUTELY ANOTHER

ALLENTOWN ANGLOPHILE "AGA

ALLENTOWN ANGLOPHILE
THE KINGS RANSOM
THE SHILLINGS
THE LIMITS
JAY & THE TECHNIQUES
BLEU GRASS

1. Kings Ransom - Shame - (Hamick/Marloy) - Integra Music BMI
2. Kings Ransom - Here Today, Gone Tomorrow - (Dougherty/Jobs)
3. Kings Ransom - Unknown To Me - (Kings Ransom)
4. Kings Ransom - Without You - (Kings Ransom)
5. Limits - He'll Make You Cry - (James Eyan) - Tender Tunes BMI
6. Limits - The Key - (Gene Jones) - Flying Governor Music BMI
7. Limits - Just What I Need - (Dirk Lerry) - Flying Governor Music
8. Jay & The Techniques - Soft Drink Commercial #1
9. Jay & The Techniques - Soft Drink Commercial #2
10. Shillings - Laugh - (Mark Jennings, Jr.) - Morris Music BMI
11. Shillings - Lyin And Tryin - (Tom Ross) - Pronto Music BMI
12. Shillings - Children & Flowers - (Deshannon) - Emi Unart
13. Shillings - The World Could Stop - (Jennings/Ross)
14. Shillings - Loving Spell - (Jennings/Ross)
15. Shillings - I'll Get To You - (Jennings/Ross)
16. Shillings - Seems Like Yesterday - (Jennings/Ross)
17. Dooley Invention - Crimson Afternoon - (Jennings/Ross)
18. Dooley Invention - No Time - (Jennings/Ross)
19. Bleu Grass - What I Know - (Rob Freeman) - Monster Pup BMI
20. D.B.L.I.T.Y. - Go West Young Man - (Gant/Noxious)
21. D.B.L.I.T.Y. - Cut My Hair Today - (R. Gant)

©2005 DISTORTIONS   WWW.DISTORTIONSRECORDS.COM

THE OREDAD

Hailing from the Lehigh Valley area, The Oredad were the classic garage/basement band as the photos will show. These guys practiced in their basement. Can you imagine what mom & pop said when they were trying to watch Walter Cronkite or Lawrence Welk on the TV.

The Oredad were Jim Nastasee (RIP), Ken Siftar, Terry "McGraw"Palmer and Frank Nastasee. This was in their high school days when these guys were still raw musicians and learning their riffs. But practice, practice, made them what they were. Influenced by groups like Eric Clapton and Cream, some Mersey Beat and the folksy sounds of the Lovin Spoonful, the Oredad put together a very respectable list of songs for their gigs. Some of the members went on to other bands down the road.

The Oredad - Mid 60's Jim Nastasee (RIP), Ken Siftar, Terry"Mcgraw"Palmer, Frank Nastasee

Oredad Terry Palmer, Jim Nastasee(RIP), Frank Nastasee and Ken Siftar probably playing some Cream or Lovin Spoonful

Frank Nastasee on the strat and Terry Palmer on the skins in the basement of 51 W Broad ST in 1969

CHAPTER 2: REGIONAL GARAGE BANDS

THE DEVILS

Located in the Stroudsburg area, The Devils were the pride of Monroe County. Inspired by the music of Buddy Holly, Little Richard and Fats Domino, they played their tunes many an evening at The Charcoal Hearth on Rte 611(now called Studebakers). The band wrote a single called "Devil Dance" took it to a small studio in the Scranton area and made 500 copies and put it in local record stores like Speedy's in Allentown where it sold out quickly and the demand for the song was high. Local radio stations were playing the song which then was heard by DJ Gene Kaye and he took them to the Cameo/ Parkway Studios in Philly where they re-recorded the song using the names of different cities for the national exposure.

The Devils: Neil Leister, Bob McNulty (hidden) Ed Hill, Bob Weidner

The Devil's

the self-produced 45 "The Devil Dance"

Joe Madura at the mix console of Cameo – Parkway Studios in Philadelphia

THE KIT KATS

The Kit Kats are a Philadelphia area band formed in 1962. Their early style was a mixture of doo-wop and soul which later evolved to baroque rock. Although the Kit Kats were very popular locally, they did not chart nationally until 1966 with "Let's Get Lost on a Country Road."

The Kit Kats changed their name to New Hope in 1969 and their best known song, "Won't Find Better than Me", made the Billboard Hot 100 in 1970.

The Kit Kats at The Cameo in Allentown in 1970

THE NAZZ

The Nazz were a legendary late 60's Philly quartet who's guitarist and main songwriter was Todd Rundgren. Robert "Stewkey" Antoni was the lead singer and "voice "of probably one of the best garage bands ever to come out of the Philly area. Along with Craig Bolan from the Munchkins and Greg Simpler, they put together a sound that is still viable today.

They had 2 big hits, "Open Your Eyes" went national and was an underground smash and their follow up song " Hello, It's Me" made Billboards Top 20 and is still played on radio today

THE TUMBLERS

The Tumblers from East Stroudsburg....The incredible "Scream" was 'written' by Larry La Spina, and backed with a desultory ballad, "Make You All Mine", another La Spina original. The record was cut in 1965. Larry and the band were all from the Poconos in the East Stroudsburg area. They mostly played local resorts and clubs during that period. The record was briefly a top ten hit locally and in the Allentown area

THE VESTELLS

The Vestells were a trio from around Stroudsburg, northeast of Allentown. The members were two brothers, Bob and John Schick along with C. Whitmore. They cut their only record at Cameo-Parkway studios in Philadelphia in 1966. All three were drafted the following year into the Armed Forces. This particular song ended up on a couple of garage bands compilations.

THE LEGIONS

The Legions were from the Greater Philly Area. The band was made up of school friends and played mainly high school dances, radio station hops, churches and fire hall socials. The band entered a battle of the local bands garage contest at WFIL and won. Their record "She's Gone" was a favorite among the school kids of the day. The band was influenced by the sounds of The Monkees, Paul Revere and The Raiders, The Beatles and The Beach Boys.

The Legions are Mitch Schecter – drums & vocals,
Jeff Chadrow - guitar & vocals
Walt Barr – guitar & vocals
Ed Blumenthal – organ, Ron Gordon - bass

THE RISING TIDES

In 1967, Disco Scene, a local music magazine for teens in the Delaware Valley, predicted that The Rising Tides would have a great future. The band recorded a single "Artificial Peace and Don't Want You Around" at Sound Plus Studios in Philadelphia. They appeared on many local radio and TV shows such as Ed Hurst's Steel Pier Show. They became popular in this part of the country, but never went national. The Rising Tides played the Philly scenes DJ hops and other local venues, going into the Reading area and as far south as the Jersey Shore.

STAN AND THE CAPRIS

Hailing from the Shenandoah area of Schuylkill County, Stan & the Capris used the influences of The Beatles, Rolling Stones, Elvis, The Everly Brothers and The Brit Invasion in composing their music and setlists. Working out of an old 59 Ford Fairlane Station Wagon, the band made the rounds in the region playing dances at schools, fire companies and radio DJ gigs. Their big break came when they appeared on WNEP TV 16 in the Wilkes-Barre/Scranton area.

Members of the band included:
Stan Jakaitis – vocals & rhythm guitar
Frank Malia – vocals & lead guitar
Joe Gawrylik – vocals & guitar
Jim Dunlap – vocals & keys
Bobby Green – drums.

THE MISFITS

The Misfits from the Poconos area played a mixture of music that ranged from Young Rascals to the groovy sounds of Vanilla Fudge. Mix in the Motown Sound and the Soul Survivors and you have a group that was very well rounded for the times. The band started playing in high schools, at private parties, colleges, YMCA's and formal dances and graduated to clubs like The Mod Mill and Dimensions in NYC. A big break for the band came when they were invited to play on WNEP 16's teen dance show called "Kokomotion". The Misfits were also #1 in WKAP's Allentown Fair ratings and advertised Fender Amps for Circle Music in Easton. The band consisted of Jim Young – Hammond Organ, Skip Romagnoli – lead guitar, Mike Takacs – bass, Jamie Takacs – drums.

The Misfits tour bus

CHAPTER 3: LEHIGH VALLEY AREA BANDS– MID 70'S TO 1990

With the music beginning to change and evolve once again, new influences were making their way into the rock club scene. AOR or Album Oriented Rock was making inroads on the FM dial. By 1975 many of the stations were moving to institute programming rules with a "clock" and system of "rotation". With this shift, Stations formats in the mid 1970s were now billed as Progressive. DJs still had much input over the music they played, and the selection was deep and eclectic, ranging from folk to hard rock with other styles such as Jazz fusion occasionally thrown in. The "rock" in album-oriented rock came in the late 1970s, when AOR music libraries and playlists discarded the wide range of genres embraced earlier on to primarily focus on a rock-centric sound. AOR formats became tighter and song selection shifted to the Program Director or Music Director, rather than the DJ. Still, when an AOR station added an album to rotation they would often focus on numerous tracks at once, rather than playing the singles as they were individually released. Local station WZZO started with this format in 1975 and still uses it today.

As more album cuts were being played on the radio, bands started to pick up on this heavier sound and moved it more into the mainstream. Such national acts as Head East, REO Speedwagon, Styx, Emerson, Lake & Palmer, Loverboy, Truimph, Billy Squire, Kansas, Heart, Genesis, Asia, Journey, Queen, Supertramp, Rush, Boston, Foreigner, Blue Oyster Cult, Cheap Trick and Steely Dan fell into AOR mold.

These new influences brought a plethora of cover bands to the Lehigh Valley club scene. This was probably the biggest upsurge in music in the Valley ever. While the cover bands were gaining popularity, bands doing their own original sounds took it on the chin as club owners booked the bands that played the more popular songs and what their crowds would relate to.

The big hair/hard rock era of rock in the 80's was also a viable outlet for music. Cinderella, Quiet Riot, Poison, Warrant, AC – DC, Sammy Hagar, Twisted Sister, David Lee Roth, Van Halen, Guns N Roses, Metallica, Iron Maiden, Judas Priest and the Scorpions were some of these bands.

It wasn't until about 1983 – 84 that original music from local bands started to make a comeback. Certain clubs and coffeehouses would cater to these new original bands as a way to save money over the cover bands whose prices had risen to new heights. Thus a new alternative/rock/new wave/ska/punk type sound emerged and gained national prominance. Some radio stations like WIFI 92 in Philadelphia catered to this new sound which made its move to the mainstream.

Bands in this genre included the Flock of Seagulls, The Cure, Soft Cell, the Thompson Twins, Duran Duran, The Fixx, Squeeze, Devo, INXS, OMD, ABC, New Order and Frankie Goes to Hollywood.

From dance rock to hard rock to punk to alternative, The Lehigh Valley was alive with music and people started to take notice. The club scene was jumpin and new venues were being created to handle this upswing in music. From the small 40 seat joint to the 1000 person concert halls, we were enjoying this selection of music that was available to us on a daily basis. These bands ran the gamut of styles from covers to originals to just plain noise. I enjoyed watching and listening to new bands together for a month and wet behind the ears to the seasoned veterans and their polished sounds go on stage and pour their hearts out to the gathered masses. Some bands had followings and fans, others were just a small group of friends. Whatever the band, wherever the club, I always enjoyed the sounds of that days rock and roll. This chapter is probably the largest collection of Lehigh Valley bands that will ever be presented to the masses. In no particular order, I will try to present this era of music that will satisfy everyone.

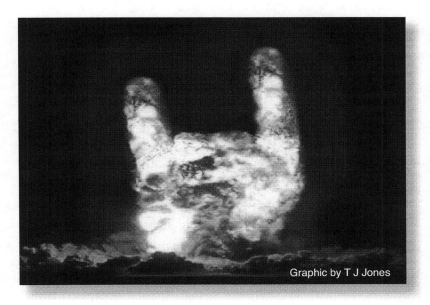

Graphic by T J Jones

Bands from the 1975 to 1990 include Magnum, Gandalf, Trust, Vagabond, T Roth & Another Pretty Face, BamBam, Family Of Strangers, Daddy Licks, Crisis, Witness, Fury, The Sharks, The Skam, The Blissters, Tikit, Triplum, Beru Revue, Ultra, Roughhouse/Teeze, Borzoi, Hybrid Ice, St John's Alliance, Idle Threats, Bullet, Magenta, Tangier, Alien, Pegasus, Flamin Harry, Destroyer, Dirty Blonde, Kraken, Leviathan, Sapient, Harpo, Money, Cheeter, Johnny's Dance Band, Rasputin, Triad, Nasty Nasty, EndZone, The Breaks, The Front, Scott Hott Band, Egdon Heath, Aviator, Bricklin, Electric City, Holland Blondes, Simon Apple, Shea Quinn Band, Senate, Duke, Howe II, Caragher-Murphy Band, Maize, Dead End Kids, Kings & Queens, Syn, The Results, Trendsetters, The Jets, The Shouts, 2+2, Albeck Brothers, Ralph, The BBC, Black Rose, PF and Men Out Of Work, Gallivant, Oasis, Wild Bill & The Back Seat Drivers, Gypsy Souls, Byron Grey, Dave Fry, Craig Thatcher, Jim Loftus, John Gorka, Nobody's Heroes, Snoblind, The Flamin Caucasians, Joey Saint, Ruby, Riff Raff, Landslide, Marmalade, Washed, Paragon, Sizzler, Strange Brew, The Zees, Trance, Le Cause, Barnaby Plum, Rampage, Christian, The Blessing, Vicious Barreka, Replacements, TT Quick, White Hott, Sweet Tequila, Follow Fashion Monkeys, Mugface, Treason, Fractured Seconds, The Rebeltones, Steve Brosky, Fuzzy Bunny, Energy and more.

MAGNUM

Magnum was formed in May of 1978 by Lonnie Warner and Steve Weiss, formerly of the popular dance group Trust, with the help of Dave Sestak of Media Five Entertainment. They teamed up with former Auburn member Butch Samolewicz, Dave Werkheiser of Oasis, Charlie Lippincott of Kydds and bass player, sound and light man Rico Corcoran. Tommy Zito was a later addition on keys & vocals. Magnum debut in July of 1978, and overnight established themselves as one of Lehigh Valleys favorite bands. Later in 1978 they expanded their appearance schedule, gaining fans and building a professional reputation throughout Eastern Pennsylvania and New Jersey. Magnum was Voted #1 rock band, in the annual rock Poll in the spring of 1979, conducted by WZZO-FM 95, Bethlehem, PA

Magnum has had many personnel changes throughout the years, but still has maintained that highly polished edge that made them a crowd favorite wherever they played. From the Lehigh Valley to the Jersey Shore to Florida, they are still very popular.

Magnum was part of the Miller Rock Network of bands and was on their tour in the early 80's. They appeared on the WPHL-17 TV Show "Dancin On Air " live on the beach in NJ and were part of a live broadcast from the Empire Rock Room in Philly on Joe Bonodano's show on WMMR.

Public Memory #1 the first single from the album "Hot Nights", was picked by Billboard Magazine in the October 8, 1983 issue as having the potential to reach the Top 30. At the same time Public Memory #1 was on the play lists of radio stations in Pa, NJ, MD and Delaware.

These guys also were practical jokers. One evening Davey Werkeiser went up on the roof of the Rock Palace and painted "Home of Magnum" on the Rock Palace sign, Bill Daniels flipped. Other antics include Butch going around with a chainsaw when the band played "Psycho Killer' and Davey running thru the crowd on roller skates when the band played "Move It On Over", "Keep You Hands To Yourself" and "Let The Good Times Roll" The funniest thing had to be when the members of the band brought a LIVE raccoon named Wilbur on stage and jammed with him.

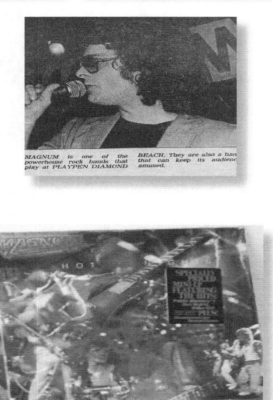

MAGNUM is one of the powerhouse rock bands that play at PLAYPEN DIAMOND BEACH. They are also a band that can keep its audience amused.

GANDALF

Gandalf was one of those bands that once you heard them, you went back for more. Their renditions of Head East's "Since You've Been Gone" and "Never Been Any Reason" and REO Speedwagon's "Keep on Rollin" still resonate today. As one of the Valley's most popular bands, they played some of the hottest clubs from The Rock Palace to The Firehouse to The Jersey Shore. A reunion is planned for this year.

JOHNNY DEE   MANAGEMENT

Gandalf

Media 5

SUITE 600
1st NATIONAL BANK BUILDING
FOURTH & NORTHAMPTON ST
EASTON, PA
(215) 258-2308

Gandalf is Ernie Kortvely, Tommy Ference Chuck Hoerl, Greg Roth

#1 ROCK BAND
Z-95 1982 ROCK POLL

GandalF
The Ultimate Party Band

Gandalf: Greg Roth, Ernie Kortvely, Chuck Hoerl, Tommy Ference and Wasa Wasa

TRUST

Trust was one of those good funky get down rock and roll bands. Though they were short lived, they were well received every time they played onstage. They were a band that knew how to jam and make people move their feet on the dance floor. They played clubs like Odysseus, Scarlett O Hara's, The Firehouse, The Rock Palace. The Lighthouse and many other Lehigh Valley gin joints on the club circuit.

This band was the father of a few other bands that went on to bigger and better things like Borzoi and Magnum, which was the thing back in those days. A lot of bands like Trust spun off and the members joined other acts.

T ROTH & ANOTHER PRETTY FACE

Where do I start here? This band was a show band. Their music was designed to mesmerize their fans and listeners. Terry Roth had such a dynamic voice that he would be an actor onstage and pour his heart into his music. His rendition of David Bowie's "Space Oddity" along with other David Bowie standards together with his costumes and makeup were totally unique for the time. He was almost a one man show! I did a gig opposite this band on New Year's Eve 1974 at Odysseus and it was a night I shall never forget. It ranks as one of the 5 best nights I ever had in a club in my lifetime.

l-r Paul Brazzo, T. Roth, Carl Brazzo, Rob Nevitte and Charles Peer.

A little bit of history of the band. APF was born in 1972 in Easton PA as a bunch of Lafayette College student got together to see where this enterprise would take them. They wanted to be more than a "Chicago" type coverband, they wanted to be unique, different and memorable. They all lived together on a farm in Bangor and rehearsed relentlessly. They played Allentown's infamous Cameo Lounge which led them to their manager who took them to a new level playing clubs from Fort Lauderdale to Ontario, Canada. After those gigs, they played in NYC at Club 82 which was frequented by David and Angela Bowie and John Lennon. The rest is history. After that, the band incorporated an entire set of David Bowie music into their show which gained them kudos from the industry and entertainment gurus.

A collection of Another Pretty Face LP releases

WITNESS

During the late 1970's, 1980's and early 1990's, there was a certain band that took the Lehigh Valley, Philadelphia and the Jersey Shore by storm. This band was Witness. The gigs were a blast, people partied to the max and the band played excellent classic rock and roll. To this day, I still listen to the cassette tape I have of them recorded at the Rock Palace in 1978 of Witness doing their signature Jethro Tull & Genesis shows, complete with flute and effects that if you close your eyes and not know it was a cover band, sounds like the real thing live.

Yes, they had that effect on you. They were perfectionists but they still had lots of fun doing it.

Witness is: Michael La Buono on keys & vocals, Roy Altemus on bass & vocals, Flip Britton on sax, flute, bass, guitar & vocals, Marc Britton on lead guitar, sax & vocals, Mitch Schecter on drums and Billy Spence on vocals

Billy Spence

Mitch Schecter

Flip Britton

Roy Altemus

Mike LaBuono

Mark Britton

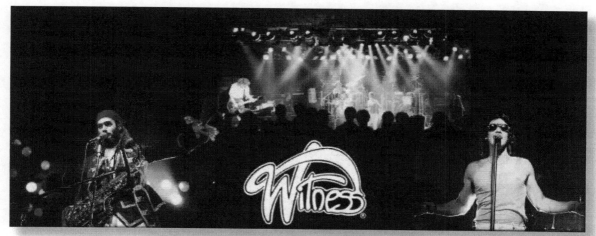

91

FUZZY BUNNY

Fuzzy Bunny was a good-time, get-down, funky party band that played the Lehigh Valley Area in the mid 70's. Led by the dynamic frontmen of Emmitt Harris and Mookie Wilson, the Bunny packed dance floors and energized crowds with their dance hits and party tunes of the day.

I first saw the Bunny at Jerry Deane's Phase V Disco in Bethlehem, PA on a small stage that the band barely fit on, but they still jammed and partied. They also played local clubs like the Green Pine Inn and Dukes Pub in Allentown, The Lighthouse and Mr Cips in Bethlehem and The Firehouse in Easton. Regional clubs included The Silo in Reading, The Inferno in Ashland, Conn's Garden in Shamokin and Frankie's Place in Philly. They also played at The Hurricane in Ocean City, MD, Daddy's in DC and Jerry Blavat's Memories in Margate, NJ.

They also played concerts as an opening act for such acts as Wild Cherry, Vickie Sue Robinson, The Village People and Chuck Berry. I had the privilege of accompanying them to Gus Genetti's in Wilkes-Barre, PA when they opened for Tavares.

They also made numerous TV appearances on such shows as the WFIL TV Variety Club Telethon, The Ed Hurst Steel Pier Show from Atlantic City, NJ and The Jerry Blavat Show where they appeared with Sammy Davis JR.

The Original Fuzzy Bunny
From left to right: Chuck Hoey (drums), Alex Gergar (keyboards), Emmitt Harris (vocals)
Mook Stanton (vocals) Dave Kapalko (lead guitar and vocals), Ron Billie (bass guitar)

EQUINOX

l to r: Tony Tarole - drums & vocals, T Bone Bauer - bass, Steve Valek, Tom Nicholson - keys & vocals, Mario "Chief" Garcia, Raymond Tyler – vocals

INTRO

Equinox is the time when the sun's center crosses the equator causing equal length of both day and night. Such an event is truely unique, as is the band which carries it's name! Equinox combines popular funky music with dynamic visuals to create an extremely professional show.

PERSONNEL

T. Bone Bauer — bass & percussion
Mario "Injun" Garcia — vocals, congas, timbales, & assorted percussion
Tom Nicholson — vocals, piano, organ, & synthesizers
Tony Tarole — vocals & drums
Ray Tyler — vocals & percussion
Steve "Dr. Von" Valek — vocals & guitar

MATERIAL

Equinox has a fine blend of current Top 40 songs recorded by such artists as:

Isley Bros.	Average White Band	Traveres
Earth, Wind & Fire	Hall & Oates	Tower Of Power
Blackbyrds	Pointer Sisters	Orleans
Doobie Bros.	Crusaders	Wings
Peoples Choice	Roberta Flack	War
KC & The Sunshine Band	Sly Stone	Labelle
Eagles	Eddie Harris	Harold Melvin & The Bluenotes

REFERENCES

If references concerning Equinox are desired, contact Denny Somach (c/o radio station WSAN, Allentown, Pa.) or Jerry Dean (c/o Phase 5 Discotheque, Bethlehem, Pa.).

RECOMMENDED FORMAT

Due to the quality and type of material performed by the band, they are recommended for any situation where live entertainment is required!

For further information
and/or promo material
contact

EQUINOX

407 Oakwood Drive
Whitehall, Pa. 18052

(215) 433-1835
(215) 432-5423

Equinox Bio

FIASCO

Blair Pipinger-vocals, Ray Tyler-vocals, Paul Coles-drums, Dan Frederick-guitar, Dave Frederick-bass, Greg Scott-horns, Bob Shemeneck-trumpet, Craig Kastelnik-keyboards.

FIASCO

Dan Frederick
(215) 435-4925

Bill Lapsansky
(717) 394-3668

Fiasco opening for the James Gang

BUTTON

clockwise from bottom left: Steve Valek, Joe "Fats" Benkovic - guitar, Peaches "LeMans" Jones - vocals, Craig Coyle - vocals & drums, Lynette McKeever - vocals, Willie Pratt – bass

HYBRID ICE

Hybrid Ice has gone through many changes in its lifetime. From the high school years in the early 70's to the late 80's, the band changed, grew and matured. Their name came to them in a weird way. They wanted something different. Other bands in the period had names that sounded interesting, were catchy, but didn't mean a damn thing. One day, drummer, Rick Klingler, came into a rehearsal with a name "The Hybrid Ice Company" Over the years, the name was shortened to Hybrid Ice and to fans they were just known as The Ice. The band made history after the release of their first album by being the first rock band to ever play at the regions largest outdoor event, The Bloomsburg Fair. This is the first time a local act played the fair in its 120 year history and set the stage for years to come. During their reign, the band opened for such national acts as Foreigner, Kansas, Bad Company, Joan Jett, Toto, Steppenwolf, Edgar Winter, Todd Rundgren, The Beach Boys, Lita Ford and Ted Nugent. Boston recorded one of their songs named "Magdalene" and renamed it "Amanda".

Hybrid Ice's lineup for 13 years was Galen Foulke, Jeff Willoughby, Rick Klinger, Chris Alburger and Bob Richardson.

Hybrid Ice 1975

Hybrid Ice in the early 80's

No Rules LP   Hybrid Ice LP

PEGASUS

Pegasus was another of the big hair cover rock bands that played the local Lehigh Valley club circuit. From the Firehouse to the Rock Palace to The Silo, they had an energy that was all the rage. Their ability to take a rather hard cover song and convert it into a danceable jam tune made them favorites of the party scene and their looks made the ladies scream. Every once in a while the occasional pair of panties or a bra would land on the stage. Pegasus recorded an original single entitled "A Heartbeat Away" & "Don't Talk to Me" on Upstage Records. I used to have a lot of fun watching these guys jam and play all the hot cover tunes of the day to the delight of the ladies in the crowd. Roger Girke went on to other bands after the demise of the group.

BAM BAMM

Purists of TV need not know where the name of this band came from. If you watched The Flintstones back in the day, you'll know Bam Bamm was Barney & Betty's son. **Bam Bamm** burst upon the scene in the mid 70's as a party cover band that rocked the house. With music from Foreigner, Reo Speedwagon and a host of others, this band rocked venues like Odysseus, The Rock Palace/Music Factory, The Castle Inn and others. These guys always gave it up when they were on stage and never failed to impress. At the end of the night, they didn't want to leave the stage either and would have kept playing if there wasn't a LCB curfew.

Tommy Ference - Drums
Tommy Giovarelli - Bass, Vocals
Tim Coval - Guitar, Vocals
John Ortiz - Lead Vocals

DADDY LICKS

Probably one of the most prolific bands from the late 70's and 80's, Daddy Licks was "THE" prototype of a high energy original music act to ever hit the Lehigh Valley. Their ballsy brand of R & B rock made them one of the top draws ever to play the area. The originality in their music has been well documented and their recordings have acclaimed fame and kudos wherever they played. Under the direction of Dave Goddess, Daddy Licks has persevered for over 30 years.

The highly acclaimed EP " I Got Wheels was released in 1981. The tracks on this EP are Valley standards today. The tracks include " We'll Show 'Em", "Just A Little (Goes A Long Way)", "They Might Be Giants" (which predates the band of the same name), "Lolita", the title track " I Got Wheels", " Tragic Flaw" and " Kids Out Looking For The Real Thing".

No one quite remembers whose idea it was to ask Scott Hott to join the Daddy Licks Band in late 1980. But now, more than a quarter-century later, Daddy Licks mainstays Dave and Kevin Goddess and onetime manager Bill Villa all agree that getting the guitarist into the Allentown rock band was both a crucial decision and a delicate matter. "When he was asked to join, he was emerging as a big force, the best guitar player in town," says Villa. "We knew Scott was a real talent, but didn't know how well he would mesh," notes drummer Kevin Goddess in a separate interview.

DON'T BE A WIMP
PLAY IT LOUD

Daddy Licks Live Album

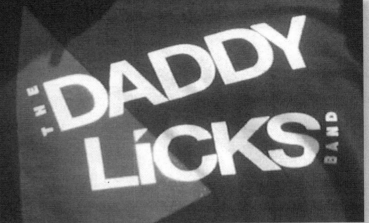

The late, great, Scott Schneck, AKA Scott Hott

FURY

Fury was a local band that played most Lehigh Valley area rock clubs. Fury was a regular at Mickey Kelley's East, the Rock Palace, Firehouse, Lighthouse. Steve Weiss, formerly with Magnum, brought his fiery interpretation of a rock guitarist to Fury to propel them into the Valley's rock scene. Fury was only around a few years, but they left a lasting impression on many of their fans.

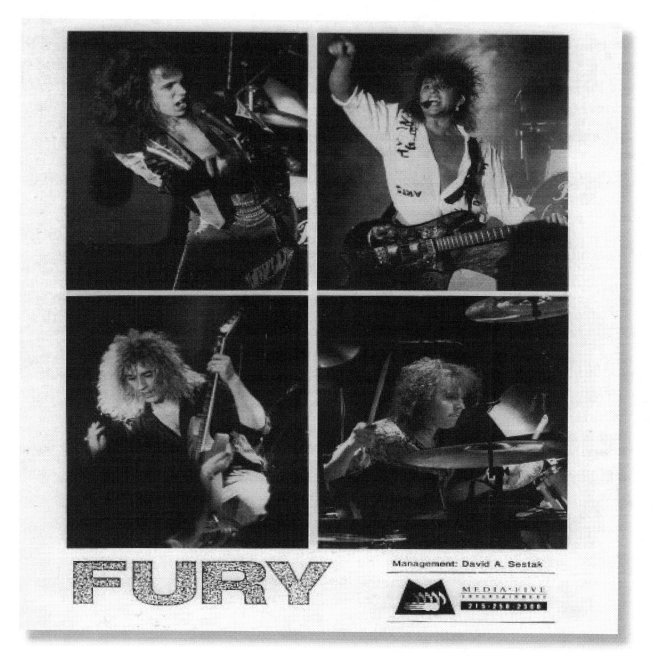

THE SHARKS

The Sharks are a new wave band founded in Lancaster, Pennsylvania in 1979, by Doug Phillips (drums, vocals), Steve Zero (guitar), Sam Lugar (guitar, vocals), and Dave Schaeffer.

The band members started by playing cover versions of songs by new wave artists such as Elvis Costello, U2, and Talking Heads, but soon progressed to performing their own material as The Sharks. The band built up a regular following of fans playing gigs up and down the East coast, and their first single caught the ear of Billy Terrel, who asked the band to record a cover of "Fly Like an Eagle" for the Philadelphia Eagles Super Bowl XV team. This led to a guest spot on "AM Philadelphia "and gigs at venues such as New York's CBGB's.

They won MTV's Basement Tape Competition in late 1986 by the largest margin in the history of the MTV Basement Tape Competition, leading to a four-EP contract with Elektra Records, who immediately put The Sharks into RPM Studios and The Power Station in NYC to record *In A Black and White World* which featured "On My Own" and "Only Time Will Tell". Videos for both songs were shot on location in Times Square in NYC. "Only Time Will Tell" was the second most requested song during MTV's Top 10 Countdown for 2 weeks in a row in 1988. With the success of the Elektra release and the support of MTV, the Sharks toured and shared the stage with The Go-Go's, A Flock of Seagulls, Robert Palmer, Joan Jett and The Blackhearts, The Romantics, Night Ranger, The Fixx, and The Stray Cats. The band had a falling out with Elektra, but continued to tour and record. In 1986 Guitarist Steve Zero, was replaced by Philadelphia based guitarist, Roger Girke, who had previously been with Robert Hazard, The Front and Pegasus. Girke stayed with the band until his departure in 1989. With 12 successful years and a lifetime of great memories, The Sharks decided to call it quits in 1992, when they realized that Elektra records was not holding up to their promise. The Sharks, with members Shea Quinn, Sam Lugar, Doug Phillips, Mark Showers and Steve Zero, have reunited yearly at the Village Nightclub in Lancaster, Pennsylvania for reunion concerts, where the band started. Schaeffer is a music teacher for the ELCO Middle school and Girke has been an active blues performer since 1990.

On October 8, 2009, lead singer, Sam (Lugar) Rawhauser, died of lung cancer.

Sharks

SHEA QUINN   SAM LUGAR   DOUG PHILLIPS   MARK

ST JOHN'S ALLIANCE

St John's Alliance was formed in the summer of 1983 by two high school pals, Jon McNamara (a good witch) and Ron Vail (a right mean cow) when they discovered how much fun it was to harmonize while singing songs by Lennon/McCartney. They even took a crack at writing their own songs like their fab hero's and made sure that almost every song had a nice harmony and that thing they called "the sound", which seemed to mean jangly guitars and lots of minor chord progressions. This made their songs sound happy and sad at the same time, thus confusing their listeners and made them come back the following weekend to give it another go. Drummer Dennis Eisenhart was also a school mate who loved bug music and it wasn't long before the trio had attracted the talents of a handsome young cat named Ken Bussiere. Ken is a fab bass player and lover of good music (Kaja-Goo-Goo, Lionel Ritchie, Clay Aiken...) and was a major force in the 'education' of his fellow band mates when it came to the more obscure music of their favorite period, the 60's. The band debut was the fall of 1983 as an opener for legendary local rockabilly raves, "The Rebeltones". Both bands hit it off swimmingly and a good time was had by all that chilly night at the 2nd Avenue in Bethlehem, Pa. ST John's Alliance also played Club PASCAL and the Airport Music Hall on numerous occasions and was always the crowd favorite. The band released a couple of EP's that still get airplay on the local college stations.

Morning Call photo—Burt Swayze

ST. JOHN'S
ALLIANCE

THE TRENDSETTERS

The Trendsetters was one of those bands that wherever they went, people followed. They had a unique original garage type sound that propelled them to become Valley favorites in a very short time "Set the Trend" which was released in '81, was dedicated to John Lennon, he was murdered on a night that the band was mixing down the record.

The Trendsetters are Mike Stanley, Kevin Shire, Ron Sabol(Ronnie Rock) and they called Bethlehem , Pa home.

The "Set the Trend" EP featured the tracks "We Are Young", "Pressure", "Catholic Girls" & "Born to Follow"

The Trendsetters were Valley favorites and played such clubs as 2ⁿᵈ Avenue, The Funhouse, Club PASCAL, Airport Music Hall as well as many other venues.

Ron Sabol - aka Ronnie Rock - The Trendsetters

FLAMIN' HARRY BAND

The Flamin' Harry Band is a trio of home-grown musicians stripping down rock 'n' roll to its basics: a pounding beat, a flurry of bluesy guitar riffs and a stinging yet plaintive human voice communicating only the most primal emotions. It's a style of music that Philadelphia area-based recording artist Flamin' Harry describes simply as "rock that hasn't sold out." After enduring years of tedious synthesizer bands and whining boys of summer, the uncompromised rock 'n' roll of The Flamin' Harry Band is a welcome addition to the music scene.

I remember seeing Harry for the first time in 82 at Hideaway Park in Bethlehem and was totally blown away by his sound. This is the type of band that you drank shots of Jack Daniels and got into the jams and went home feeling so great afterwards. Harry McGonigle is a blues-rock artist from the Philly area that fits right in with the tradition of George Thorogood and his Delaware Destroyers.

CRISIS

Crisis was an awesome reggae/ska/alternative party band. During their years playing in the Lehigh Valley, Crisis would jam to the tunes of the English Beat, Bob Marley and The Wailers, Third World Band, The Specials and Madness. Mix in U-2 and The Police with Sting and you had a well rounded get down party band.

I first heard Crisis at Hideaway Park in Bethlehem, and was so impressed by their sound that I asked them to open my first venture in concert promoting at Muhlenberg College on March 30th, 1983 with The Romantics and Single Bullet Theory. I also worked with the band at Club PAS-CAL and The Airport Music Hall. In the summer of 1985, I restarted the Parkway concerts and Crisis was on the bill along with Daddy Licks. Their sound was extraordinary and the horns added that extra fullness that other bands of the era lacked.

Lehigh Valley band Crisis circa 1984. Pictured are Pete Cline, Bryan Schrieter, Joe Davies, Carol Alee (RIP) and 99 The Hawk's Todd Heft, and Scott Siska.

The original Crisis

Crisis at the Airport Music Hall, in this photo: Peter Cline, Scott Hott(RIP), Bryan Schrieter, Joe Davies, Carol Alee(RIP), Scott Siska & 99.9's Todd Heft.

TRIPLUM

Triplum was one of those Valley bands that didn't fit into a mold. They were a band all their own and their music proved that fact. In August of 1980, enamored by well-meaning promises of Bob Maicks, they moved back to the Lehigh Valley to be closer to New York and Philly. To "bump up" the sound a little, the band decided to add bass and drums. Chuck on bass was a shoo-in, but they held many auditions for drummers until they finally found Don Jarmoska. "Jarmo" fit in personally and musically quite well, and the Lehigh Valley version of Triplum was formed. Triplum made their debut in the Allentown Parkway in late August. The emphasis at that point was still our uniqueness: strong three-part harmony, jazz and blues influences, and a progressive style of originals in the vein of Kansas and Yes.

It was probably in 1982 that we were up against stiff competition from LV bands with heavy guitar influences. Although Dave played some guitar in the band, they needed a "real" guitarist to reproduce the current pop hits. Enter Craig Thatcher. Craig gave us the commercial sound we needed, and added an edge to the progressive genre. It was during this period that Triplum filled in for Huey Lewis and the News, opening a concert at a college in central PA for .38 Special and opened at the Lichtenstein for New Riders of the Purple Sage. The band also enjoyed working with Rogue and Witness several times.

I met the band for the first time at Hideaway Park in 1983 when I was doing DJ work there between bands and they impressed me with each number they played. Triplum were true professionals in every sense of the word and it showed in their presentation. In August of 1984 the band split up over a difference of direction, both geographical and musical.

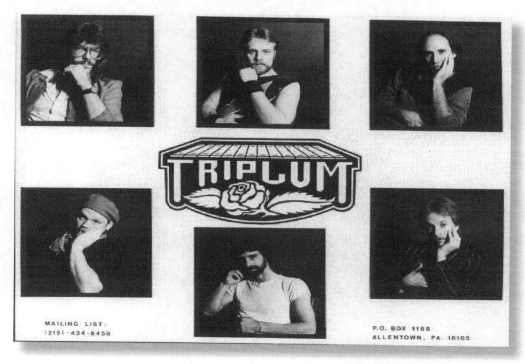

MAILING LIST:
(215) - 434 - 6456

P.O. BOX 1188
ALLENTOWN, PA. 18105

Triplum promo art

Triplum circa 1981

STEVE BROSKY

Steve Brosky grew up in the shadows of the industrial smoke stacks in the working class city of Allentown. After his years as a youth, Steve picked up the guitar and embarked on his rock and roll dream. His style of music can be described as eclectic and down to earth. When writing his songs for his various bands, he doesn't hold anything back. All his lyrics are deep felt and come from his vast range of local experiences. His bands include the Buix, the BBC, Bop Patrol, Dr Love & the Joints Jumpin and a host of solo and duo appearances.

Steve Brosky's recording career includes songs like "The Ballad of John & Yoko" inspired by the death of John Lennon in 1980, "Do The Dutch" in 1993 which became a regional hit and got kudos from many music pubs and garnered him the key to the city of Allentown by Mayor Daddona, "15th ST Blues" and "Get Out" in 1985, " Wild and Dutch" in 1986, "Any Minute Now" in 1995, "Limestone & James" in 2000 and many others.

Steve Brosky has been a staple in the Lehigh valley performing at such places as the Seemsville Inn, Club PASCAL, Musikfest, Mayfair, The Lehigh Parkway and many local and regional clubs and venues. Steve continues to perform his hits today and will be around the Valley for many years to come.

The original "Hey Man"

Dr. Love and
The Joints Jumpin'
Featuring The Lovettes

Front - Karan McGee - Steve Brosky - Vocals
Back - Pat Fioriglio - Sax, Wayne "Paco" Maura -Drums, Bobby Soul - Bass, Scott"Hott"Schneck (RIP) – Guitar ,
Rob Rhiel - Keys, Gary-Trumpet

Steve Brosky

Steve Brosky & The Bop Patrol

MAGENTA

Magenta was the area's premier all-girl band that debuted in the 80's during the resurgence of the girl bands. Bands like the Bangles, Go-Go's, Banarama, the Wilson Sisters with Heart and Wilson Philllips were definitely influences, but the ladies turned to the hard-rock boy bandsfor their sound. At the time in the early 80's, there were no other girl groups rocking out in the Lehigh Valley area.

Maureen "Moe" Jerant on drums kept a beat that was infectious and set the tone for the rest of the girls. With their guitar work and vocals, June, Beth, Gina and Ceryn gave a show which got people on the dance floor and kept the energy flowing. I first met them at Hideaway Park in Bethlehem and was impressed after the first song. The members of the band went their separate ways after breaking up with June Thomas fronting other bands and Moe Jerant working in the sound and equipment business and giving drum lessons. June Thomas and Moe Jerant are still performing today.

Magenta is June Thomas, Ceryn Iancu, Beth Boone, Moe Jerant, Gina Balducci

119

Magenta performing at the Liederkranz

SUE PERRY AND THE WILD BOYS

I first met Sue Perry many moons ago at Bill Daniel's Rock Palace before her gigging days when she was married to her husband Steve who was a friend of mine. They used to come and hear a lot of the bands that played there and we became good friends. I next saw her at Hideaway Park in Bethlehem when she fronted her band Ultra in 1983. Sue and her bands have played the Lehigh Valley area since 1983 and she is still an active performer with her band Screamin Pink and goes by the name of Alexxis Steele.

Charles Illingworth, Tim Zavar, Susan Steele, Shane Stoneback, Rich Trapp

Alexxis Steele first rocked the Valley in 1983, with her band Ultra, playing the circuit clubs, The Windsor House, DJ Bananas, Green Pine Inn, & Airport Music Hall. Bands include:

ULTRA- 1983-87
VITAL FORCE-1987-88
SUE PERRY & THE WILD BOYZ- 1988-90
CYCLONE CENTRAL- 1994-1996
DESERT RAIN-1996-1998
UNPLUGGED- 1998-1999
TOTAL PLASTIC- 1999-2001
SWETTY BETTY-2001-2003
NOBODYS BUSINESS- 2003-2004
ACOUSTIC SIGNALS- 2004-2005
BANG BANG BETTY-2005-2008
ULTRAVIOLET- 2008-2009
SCREAMIN PINK- 2009

SCOTT SCHNECK AKA SCOTT HOTT

Words cannot describe the talent that Scott Hott offered to his listeners, fans and most of all to his fellow band members. He has been described by his fellow band mates as the most talented guitarist they had ever seen in the Lehigh Valley. Daddy Licks former manager Bob Villa is quoted as saying "When he was asked to join, he was emerging as a big force, the best guitar player in town,"

Unique, talented, soft-spoken, tuned in, creative, and most of all caring, this is how I describe the Scott as I knew him. He had a wild side to him, but under all that was a heart of gold. We worked together on many occasions in many different venues like Hideaway Park, Club PASCAL, Airport Music Hall, Lehigh Parkway and Cedar Beach outdoor shows.

Scott's repertoire of band's include the Scott Hott Band, Crisis, Dr Love and the Joint's Jumpin, Big Fish Little Pond, Family of Strangers, Gypsy Souls and Daddy Licks.

As a member of the Gypsy Souls, they released "Weepin Willow Man"and "Trail of Tears". They recorded a demo "Ain't Nobody" that was never released.

Scott is sorely missed by everyone who knew him and experienced his unique style of music.

The Lehigh Valley Music Awards honored Scott by naming an award after him - The *Scott Hott* Award for Best Electric Guitarist that is presented yearly at their annual show.

Big Fish Little Pond 1989: Peter Cline, Mark Buschi, Scott "Hott" Schneck.

Family of Strangers sith Scott Schneck

THE FRONT

The Front was a local Allentown band that can be described as pop alternative rockers. During the "Rock of the 80's" craze, many bands like The Front sprang up and played the music of the day like the The Fixx, Psychedelic Furs, Simple Minds, INXS, The Producers and the like. The Front was adept in their use of originality with these covers and held the crowd from start to finish with their sound. The band played at the Music Hall, Hideaway Park, Club PASCAL, Mickey Kelly's, Hugo's, The Silo and other valley clubs and bars. The Front also played a concert in Allentown's Lehigh Parkway that had over 1000 people for the free show.

The Front- Mark Buschi, Kevin Checkett, Roger Girke, Pete Cline

The Front- Mark Buschi, Kevin Checkett, Roger Girke, Pete Cline

JOLLY ROGER

Jolly Roger formed in 1985 and had a 10 year run as one of the most successful and popular cover bands in Eastern Pa. The band performed thousands of shows and had an arsenal of over 200 songs. They shared the stage with many great acts including Foghat, The Guess Who, BTO, 38 Special, Hootie & the Blowfish, Our Lady Peace and Fuel. JOLLY ROGER released to two bodies of original music and a full length cassette entitled JOLLY ROGER .They returned to the stage in 2005 following a 10 year absence and have been performing yearly reunion shows ever since. The current line-up features original members Larry Werner on guitar and Dennis Hower on bass, Longtime JR drummer Dan Lacy behind the kit, Shane Stoneback on guitar and lead vocalist Bryan Harmony.

SAINT JOHN'S ALLIANCE

Saint John's Alliance was formed in 1983 by 2 longtime friends, Jon McNamara and John Vail. Their love of all things Beatles along with The Zombies, Kinks, Left Banke and The Hollies drew them together and made them band mates and influenced their sound. Drummer David Eisenhart also went to school with the guys and became a major force in the education of his band mates.

The band made their debut in the fall of 1983 at the 2nd Avenue club opening for Valley favorites The Rebeltones in a gig that rocked the place and had people talking for months. The band also played at The Leiderkranz, Fun House, 4 G's, Castle Garden, Club PASCAL and the Music Hall.

Mark My Words/ No One Sees

Saint John's Alliance

Saint John's Alliance at Club PASCAL

DESTROYER

Destroyer was formed in the mid 80's as a Glam Rock/ Glam Metal band that was very popular during this time frame. The big hair thing was a fad of the era that came with influences from bands like Twisted Sister, Van Halen, Poison, Motley Crue, Dokken, Ratt, Warrant, Cinderella, Whitesnake and others. Destroyer was no different. Whether they rocked out or did a ballad, they had the ladies swooning in front of the stage and the dudes slamming down beers as they jammed. These guys were a Valley Party Band with a great following and wherever they played, the ladies followed. They usually outnumbered the dudes by 2 to 1. Though their life span was short lived, they left their mark wherever they played. The Funhouse, Club PASCAL, the Airport Music Hall, DJ Bananas, Empire Rock Room and The Green Pine Inn were a few of the places that they played.

Destroyer's Mikhall Myers jammin'

RALPH

Ralph is a 10-piece horn band from the Scranton area that was formed in 1969 and was popular during the disco era of the 70's and rocked out in the 80's. The band recorded at Trident Studio in London, England, produced by C.Michael Wright and engineered by Roy Thomas Baker (Queen, Nazareth, the Cars, Ian Hunter, Nazareth, Guns N' Roses, The Who, The Rolling Stones, David Bowie, Foreigner, Journey, Pilot, Ozzy Osbourne, Mötley Crüe, T.Rex, Devo, The Stranglers, Dusty Springfield, Yes, Cheap Trick,..) Later, produced by Don Costa (Frank Sinatra, Paul Anka, Osmonds, Sammy Davis Jr, Little Anthony), they performed on the syndicated TV rock concert "Music Your My Mother".In 1978 they released single "Fly by Night/Save Me on the KMA label. Ralph has gone through many changed through the years and members of the band include Billy Lombardi, Billy Cianfichi, Bobby Tansits, Bruce Kieb, Earl Schirra, Robie Schnessel, Teddy Maus, Mark "Tex" Horowitz, Marty Golub, Joe "Rock"Santaniello, Marty Menichello, Louie Cossa, Paul Dickstein, Jeff Mitchell, Buddy Mecca, Lenie Colacino, Lee Patrick, Roy Murray, Don Williams, Dennis Fura, Wayne Maura, and Miguel "Jr." Candia.

RALPH PRODUCTIONS
617 Breck Street
Scranton, Pa. 18505

(717) 346-5615

"RALPH"

RALPH Productions
for information contact
Charles DeLorenzo
area code (607) 748 2458

TEEZE

Teeze was another of those big-hair glam metal bands that made the scene in the 80's. Teeze had always been devoted to live gigs and the lure of the road. They started playing five to six nights a week in Pennsylvania, New Jersey, Delaware, Maryland and New York. It was this dedicated commitment to heavy touring that would eventually give them a five figure mailing list/fan club base and a huge loyal following. It would also lead to the decision to start focusing on original Teeze material and re-vamping the entire stage show. Bigger hair, louder amps, tons of smoke, concussion bombs, flash pots, spinning guitars, blood spurting, hair spray and spandex, spandex, spandex......If Motley Crue owned the L.A. glam scene and had successfully released a self-financed debut album on their own label, then Teeze was their east coast rival and was about to do the same.

Teeze began 1985 by writing the songs that would eventually make up their debut album. The recording process started that summer and would stretch into October of that year before the original eight tracks were in the can. A special promo 45 seven inch single "Party Hardy"/"Going Away" was released on the group's own SMC label to press and radio in November. Intended to announce the upcoming release of the LP, the disc (complete with a picture sleeve) was only pressed in a limited edition of 500 copies and was quickly snapped up by collectors.

The boys made their first television appearance on Philadelphia's "Dancin' on Air", which was a locally produced American Bandstand clone show that featured school girls dancing to their favorite songs. It was also during this time that the band began transitioning the new songs into their regular three-set per night stage show. Before the year was out, most of the cover songs were gone and the show was trimmed down to one 90 minute blast of metal mayhem complete with local opening bands. Teeze eventually morphed into the new act Roughhouse.

TT QUICK

TT Quick is known as a popular club band in the New York, New Jersey and Pennsylvania areas. The Quick has also been known for their attack of power metal and guitar work of guitarist David Di Pietro and the powerful vocals of Mark Tornillo. David DiPietro's skills were especially singled out. As a talented guitar tutor, the man had taught both ZAKK WYLDE of the OZZY OSBOURNE band and SKID ROW's Dave Sabo. They toured with big known national acts like Queensryche, Megadeth & Motorhead just to name a few.

Their discography includes the self-titled "TT Quick", "Metal of Honor" and "Sloppy Seconds".

TT Quick at Airport Music Hall

MIKE DUGAN

ROSE ALLEY

Scott "Free" Howell, Blair Rittenhouse, Bill Kutzman, Ephraim Corsino, Mike Campbell

135

BOOMER

Rich Leone, Jimmy Bevan, Johnny Jackson, John Evans, Chris McAlpine

ALIEN

HARPO

BRIAN BORTZ

IRON BOTTOM SOUND

Management
Brian Malina
610-559-8925

P.O. Box 265
Allentown, PA 18105

NASTY NASTY

P.O. Box 265
Allentown, PA 18105

(215) 791-5596
(215) 437-2633

138

REAL TO REAL

REAL MUSIC FOR A REAL TIME

Real to Real (before they were the band Fuel)

PF AND THE FLYERS

Sam Abuschinow, John Sproat, Alan Gaumer,
Peter Fluck, Mike Krisukas

ENDZONE

POKERFACE

Poker Face first hit the Lehigh Valley in 1989 playing venues such as the Zodiac Club, Airport Music Hall, and the Club PAS-CAL. In 1992, the band released its first album, "Game of Love", and embarked on a lifelong career of music and mayhem.

Poker face is Paul Topete, Dennis Beidler, Brett Griffiths, Rich Valentin

STEPPIN OUT

Picture taken at the first Celebration Allentown that grew to be the Mayfair Arts Festival
In this photo: Reid Tre (photos), Dave Fry (photos), Jeff Biro, Denny Danko, Chris Jones
Photo by Hub Willson

JESSE WADE GANG - COUNTRY MUSIC OUTLAWS

EGDON HEATH

THE JAKE KALIGIS BAND

Dino Dilucia, Scott Siska, Jake Kaligis, Judy Brunst, Scott Williams Photo by Lisa Lake

HOLLAND BLONDE

BRICKLIN

MIKE DUGAN AND THE SURVIVAL BAND

Mike Dugan, Brian Schreiter, Dave Dionisi, Scott Siska

THE SKAM

JIM LOFTUS

DIRTY BLONDE

BORZOI

BERU REVIEW

CROSSCUT SAW   **JOHN WESLEY DICKSON**   **TOWER SUITE**

PETE CARRAGHER ROCKIN THE VALLEY

White Hott

ELECTRIC CITY

SENATE

TENTATIVE RELATIONSHIP

THE KELLY MURPHY BAND

The A's

MAIZE

MAIZE

WHITE HOTT

DICK DESTINY & THE HIGHWAY KINGS

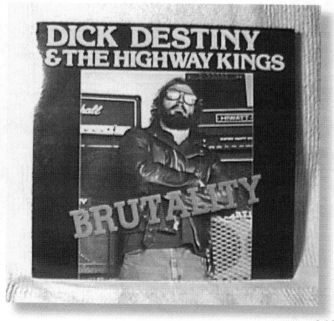

THE A'S

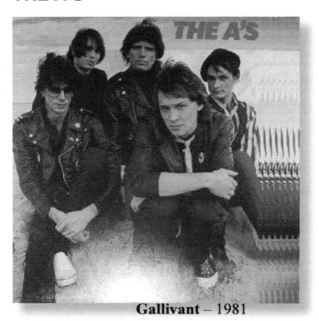

Gallivant – 1981

BLACK ROSE

1979 Jim Kahle, Peter Cline, Steve, Henry Mazepa

150

PF AND MEN OUT OF WORK (October 1983)

GALLIVANT

BYRON F. GRAY

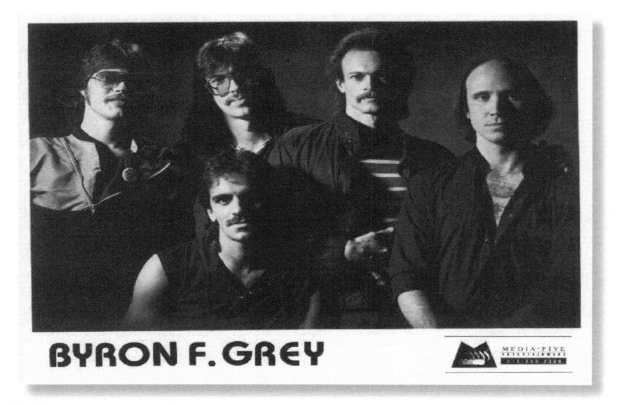

LIBRA

152

RAMPAGE

Glenn Goodge
Bass, vocals

Kevin Lang
Guitar, vocals

T. Scott Curt
Lead vocals

Tom Henning
Guitar, vocals

Dana Lang
Drums

RAMPAGE

MEDIA V entertainment

Suite 600 1st National Bank Building
Fourth and Northampton Streets
Easton, Pa. 18042
Phone 215-258-2308

DUKE

1984 Greg Howe, Al Howe, Rory Castellano, Matt Neback

OFF CENTER

1990 – Don McCord, Melissa, Larry Beahm

OASIS

NOBODY'S HEROES

SNOWBLIND

RIFF RAFF

Featuring Dan, Tom Steve and Morgan

TODD WOLF

MOB

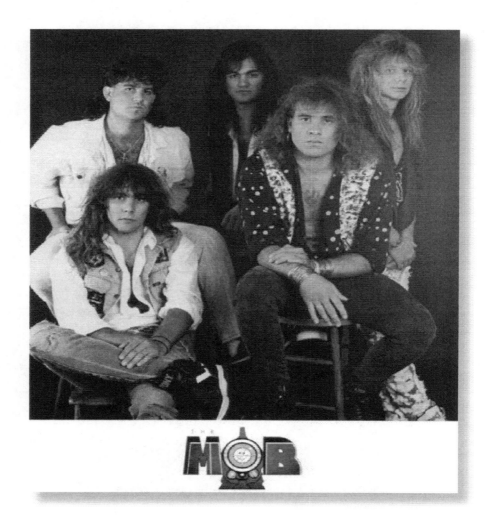

TRANCE

LANDSLIDE

PARAGON

THE ZEES

THE SURGEONS

157

STRANGE BREW

SIZZLER

JOEY SAINT

Andrew Capp, Joey Santagelo & Kirk Moyer

COUNTRY JADES

Marty -Dan Kocher-Tex Carson-Lenny D

Country Jades
Rainbow Room 1979

THE TIKIT

PAT / 215·770-0498   THE TIKIT   HUB / 215·776-0553

Hub Wilson, Pat Wallace, Gene Bloch & Christopher Jones

160

THE BLISSTERS

HARRY FISHER / The Morning Call

Ex-Blissters Doug 'Dougie Smash' Roth (left) and Scott 'Johnny Freedom' Fehnel are heading in new directions.

Doug Roth & Scott Fehnel played venues like Club PASCAL, Airport Music Hall, Funhouse & Hideaway Park

BERU REVIEW

BORZOI

162

JAY THOMAS

My good friend Jay Thomas, sound man extraordinaire, worked with many major national acts

JIMMY DELGRASSO

Drummer Jimmy Delgrasso

SHADOW GALLERY

Shadow Gallery is a six-piece American progressive metal band formed in Lehigh Valley, Penn-sylvania during the early 1980s, originally under the name Sorcerer. After changing their name to Shadow Gallery (taken from the graphic novel V for Vendetta by Alan Moore) and recording a short 8 track demo, the band was signed to Magna Carta Records in 1991. Shadow Gallery's eponymous debut was released the following year in Japan and Europe. On May 30th, 2005 (Europe) and June 7th, 2005 (USA) Shadow Gallery released their fifth studio album (Room V), their first under new record label Inside Out.

LEVIATHON

THE BLESSING

KRAKEN

FOLLOW FASHION MONKEES

THE RUSSIAN MEAT SQUATS

MAMMOTH WAIL

PHOTO BY RONN

MAMMOTH WAIL in the mid 70's

166

THE JETS

the Jets

C.K. Harris

Patti Gander, Ken Siftar, Willie Huttie, Tony Sporta & Mike Griffith

WILD BILL AND THE BACKSEAT DRIVERS

TOM WALZ

ALAN GAUMER

THAT'S US

Tom Kozic, Alan Gaumer, Migdalia Roth, John Kacmarcik, Jeff Roth

BUBBA

Jim Fedok, Allen Wolfbrandt, John Kacmarcik, Jim Gordon

169

QUICK 'N EZY

One of the pics of QUICK 'N 'EZY from the Mid 70's - they are Dave Hunsicker - drums, Curt Bayer - lead guitar, Jim Gordon(RIP) - vocals, Jim Allford - bass and comic, Bill Jones - lead guitar and Cindy Montgomery - vocals

DAVE FRY

Not enough can be said about Dave Fry. This talented musician has been entertaining in the Valley and beyond since the 60's. Dave has appeared with the bands The Shimersville Sheiks, Graveyard Skiffle Band, Pavlov's Dogs and Steppin Out in the 60's thru the 80's. His solo career is well documented also. Dave is a folksinger: adult, children's and family-music performer - arts educator/entrepreneur and good-time rascal, all rolled up in one! Dave is a mainstay as well as one of the founders of God-frey Daniel's Coffeehouse in Bethlehem. He also performs with The Touchstone Theater. Dave has performed at Mayfair and Musikfest and The Philadelphia Folk Festival..

Pavlov's Dogs " Bluegrass with Bite"

JIMMY MEYER

Jimmy Meyer has been performing in and around the Lehigh Valley over the past 20 + years. Some of the bands include: Wayne Smith Project, The Tourists, Energy, Select Four, KIK, Staples Trio, New Kind Of Talk, and currently with Steve Brosky and his Big Lil Band and Steve Brosky & Jimmy Meyer duo.

CRAIG THATCHER

Craig Thatcher has been involved with music in the area since his school days in the early 60's. his first band was in 1966 when he was only 10 yrs old. Pete played through his high school years and sat in with numerous acts including Snowball. Triad was formed in late 1974 and his career took off from there. Craigs musical taste covers a broad spectrum, from blues to jazz, 60's and early 70's rock and country artists Jerry Reed, Chet Atkins, Merle Travis, Johnny Cash, Tom Bresh. Today, Craig plays with his own band the Craig Thatcher Band and also Simone, the daughter of jazz great Nina Simone.

1966 first band

Good vibrations The rock group Triad performs at Saturday night's Back-to-School Concert held at Quakertown's Memorial Park. Shown from left are Fred W. Young, Doug McKinnon and Craig Thatcher.

Triad in 1975

Playing with Snowball in 1974

Pete Fluck & Craig Thatcher 1989

173

THE FLAMIN' CAUCASIANS

Countless fans still remember the Caucasians' gig as the house band for the popular Morning Zoo with John De Bella on Philadelphia radio station WMMR. Their energy and musical chops, as well as their spontaneity, won them the chance to "rock the house" starting at 6 AM and back up an impressive list of recording stars, comedians and celebrities, including Southside Johnny, Warren Zevon, Gregg Allman, Alan King, and Sinbad.

The Caucasians have found their way into millions of homes on local and national TV Featured on WPVIs "AM Philadelphia", they performed with comedian Big Daddy Graham. They provided musical backup in commercials for KYW Sports announcers Lou Tilley and Ukie Washington and played "Heartbreak Hotel" on a public service announcement for the Women's Humane Society.

Some of the national acts they have appeared with include: Southside Johnny, Warren Zevon, Arthur Brown, Gregg Allman, Mick Taylor, Little Feat, Mr. Big, Dave Mason, Donovan, Jon Anderson, Julian Lennon, Spencer Davis, Badfinger, The Turtles, David Bromberg, Mojo Nixon, Johnny Van Zandt, Tom Cochrane, The Smithereens, Tommy Conwell, Marshall Crenshaw, Lou Gramm, The Hooters, Robert Hazard and Pat Godwin.

KEITH JARRETT

Keith Jarrett (born May 8, 1945, in Allentown, Pennsylvania) is an American jazz icon and classical pianist and composer. Keith Jarrett graduated from Emmaus High School.

Jarrett started his career with Art Blakey, moving on to play with Charles Lloyd and Miles Davis. Since the early 1970s he has enjoyed a great deal of success in both jazz and classical music, as a group leader and a solo performer. His improvisations draw not only from the traditions of jazz, but from other genres as well, especially Western classical music, gospel, blues, and ethnic folk music.

In 2003, Jarrett received the Polar Music Prize the first (and to this day only) recipient not to share the prize with a co-recipient, and in 2004 he received the Léonie Sonning Music Prize.

In 2008, he was inducted into the Down Beat Hall of Fame by the 73rd Annual Jazz Readers' Poll.

WIILLIE RESTUM

The incomparable Willie Restum was a Jazz Maestro. He played the Lehigh Valley regions local lounges and mezmorized his crowds. Willie was a long-time resident of Allentown and made his mark with his horns. In later years, Willie went on to record many LP's and played some of the finer lounges, resorts and nightspots in the country. It was a genuine pleasure to call him friend and his performances will live in his recordings and our memories.

ROB STONEBACK'S BIG BAND

Rob Stoneback is a former member of the Tommy Dorsey, Glenn Miller and Harry James Orchestras. He is the leader, principal arranger, and featured trombonist of the Rob Stoneback Big Band.

Already known as one of the most exciting bands on the east coast, the Rob Stoneback Big Band is rapidly gaining recognition throughout the country, the band's "Up Front" album receives national airplay. The group plays the big band sounds of Glenn Miller, Tommy Dorsey, Benny Goodman etc. When Rob and the guys let it all hang out with hits from "Ghostbusters", "Huey Lewis", and "Phil Collins" look out, the place is romping!

Rob Stonebeck has performed with Sonny and Cher, Don Rickles, Steve Lawrence and Eydie Gorme, Clark Terry, Urbie Green, Bobby Watson, Wycliffe Gordon, Al Grey, Marilyn McCoo and Billy Davis Jr., Connie Stevens, and Connie Francis.

In this pic: George Grund – piano, Gary Rissmiller and Rob Stonebeck – Horns

ALLENTOWN ANGLOPHILE

This is another of the Allentown Anglophile compilations of the bands from the Lehigh Valley area that were born from the garage band era and progressed into the late 70's and 80's. You will see most of these bands in this publication.

SAINT JOHNS ALLIANCE
1. NO ONE SEES (R.Vail, J.McNamara) — 2:36
2. DON'T WANT TO WAIT (R.Vail, J.McNamara) — 2:50
3. MARYGOROUND (R.Vail, J.McNamara) — 2:48
4. MISERY ROW (R.Vail, J.McNamara) — 3:05
   Cribsong Music (ASCAP) MJP Publishing (ASCAP)

CREATURES OF THE GOLDEN DAWN
5. CRAZY DATE (C.T.) — 3:00
6. I CAN'T FIND YOU (M.Smitreski) — 2:16
7. GET ME OUT OF THIS TOWN (M.Smitreski) — 2:30

DADDY LICKS
8. CAN'T FIGHT SITTIN' DOWN (D.Goddess) — 3:36
9. WILD AND WILLING (D.Goddess) — 3:48
10. NOTHING COOL HAPPENING HERE (D.Goddess) — 3:54
11. PARADISE LOST (D.Goddess) — 4:39

SCOTT HOT BAND
12. 3 MILES HIGH (S.Schneck) — 2:38
13. HOT T' TROT (S.Schneck) — 2:42

ODDESSEY
14. NO DIVIDENDS (S.Schneck) — 4:54

SHUFFLE
15. SHADES OF HEAVEN (Arro Gant) — 4:16

THE BLISSTERS
16. ARABIAN MISSTRESS (S.Fehnel) — 3:03
17. YOU MADE ME SMILE (S.Fehnel) — 2:53

THE SKAM
18. WHAT DID I TELL HER ? (J.Rowland) — 3:33

STEVE BROSKY
19. THE BALLAD OF JOHN LENNON (Brosky, Willistein) — 3:13
   (They Finally Crucified You)

D.B.L.I.T.Y.
20. DRINKIN' CLASS HEROES (Arro Gant) — 2:53

ARRO GANT
21. WHO PUT THE WORLD IN A CAN ? (Arro Gant) — 4:22
22. LET'S HAVE A DEPRESSION (Arro Gant) — 2:16
23. BACK OUT ON THE STREET (Arro Gant) — 2:51

THE HATFIELDS AND McCOY
24. WIRE AND CONFUSION (G.McCoy) — 4:51

LEHIGH VALLEY ROCKS

Lehigh Valley Rocks is a 2-CD compilation produced by Butch Maloney and Tom LeFevre. Their dedication and hard work paid off to bring together all the talented groups/artists that have performed around the Lehigh Valley hard rock scene of 1984-1994. Thirty tracks make up this LP that will take you back to a music scene that rocked the Valley. Many of the artists have moved on to become national touring artists.

So where was Lehigh Valley and who are these artists? Lehigh Valley and their 80's hard rock metal bands where tearing up the streets too.

Bands like TEEZE "Party Hardy" a hit song that sold over 20,000 copies! SWEET TEQUILA featuring Scott Marshall/Lead vocalist-guitarist, "I Won't Be Crying". WASHED had two great songs, "Guilty" and "Alone". DESTROYER and the track "When Morning Comes" Mike Myers/lead vocalist-guitarist and Mark Bennett /drums are currently performing in the band Slik Helvetika. OMYNUS had an extremely popular draw in the clubs with their song "Don't Ever Wanna Say Goodbye" from the year of 1990. Some of you Southern California's may recognize band member Bobby Richards/drums, (Hand over Fist, Youth Gone Wild, Wood and now THE CAUSE). SAPIENT, MIZERY and DIRTY BLOND, who released 3 albums that are doing very well over seas. JOLLY ROGER with "I Won't Be Cryin", FANTAZY, THE MOB, and UNCLE REMUS with former WASHED drummer, Phil Mahr. ROCK HEAVEN, featuring bass player Matt Boyden of Treblehook. KINGS CHAMBER with Jeff Baker/bass vocals. Jeff is now performing with the classic metal tribute band DENIM AND LEATHER that features members of Metal Church, Lizzy Borden and Leatherwolf. LEVIATHEN, KRAKEN, ENDZONE, VIC MISSY, CHASER, RED OCTOBER, APATHY and SLIK HEVETIKA are a few of the other act featured here. You eighty metal lovers will want to add this to your hard rock metal music collection! You won't be disappointed.

CHAPTER 4: LEHIGH VALLEY AM RADIO

While the 1960's may have been a settled era for the vinyl recording, it was a period of massive change for the world of music, and more particular the world of radio. The transistor radio remains the single most popular communications device in existence. Some estimates suggest that there are at least seven billion of them in existence; almost all tunable to the common AM band and later models dual AM –FM band receivers. Listeners sometimes held an entire transistor radio directly against the side of the head, with the speaker against the ear, to minimize the "tinny" sound caused by the high resonant frequency of its small speaker enclosure. Most radios included earphone jacks and came with single earphones that provided only mediocre-quality sound reproduction due to the bandwidth limitation of AM (up to 10 kHz).

Transistor radios were extremely successful because of four social forces: a large number of young people, a post-World War II baby boom, a public with a disposable income amongst a period of prosperity, and the growing popularity of rock 'n' roll music. The transistor radio appeared in many popular films such as " Lolita "and the term "transistor radio" can be heard in the lyrics of Van Morrison's "Brown-Eyed Girl", a famous top 10 Billboard hit in the late 1960's.

With these new innovations came the emergence of personality radio. Looking for new ways to influence listeners radio disc-jockeys had to become more innovative and inject more of themselves into their shows Some of the early notables include Alan Freed, Cousin Brucie (Bruce

Morrow), Hy Lit, Dick Clark, Dewey Phillips, Wolfman Jack, Rick Dees, Casey Casem, Dr Donald D Rose, George Michael, Long John Wade, Don Imus, Dan Ingram and many more.

The Lehigh Valley had a host of DJ's that were part of our lives from morning till night. We would wake up in the morning and turn on the radio to hear our favorite personalities and music. WAEB, WKAP, WSAN, WHOL, WEEX, WEST, WGPA & WYNS were the Lehigh Valley AM stations of the day. We were also very fortunate to be between Philadelphia and New York City and able to listen to AM stations WFIL, WIP, WIBG, WNBC, WCBS and WABC from the big cities.

AM radio has gone thru many changes in the Lehigh Valley. Gone are the Top 40 Formats that dominated in the 60's & 70's and they are replaced by News, Polka, Oldies, Sports and Hispanic programming to fit ever changing demographics.

Jumpin Jay Sands, Ernie Steigler, Tiger Joe McClaine, Jeff Frank, Super Lou, Rod Carson, Jeff Dean, Mickey Haggerty, Frantic Freddy Frederick, Gene Kaye, Johnny Michaels, Larry Brooke, Bob Harper, Doug Weldon, Larry O Brien, Barry George, Joey Joey, Bob Wolken, Jack Burns, Alan Raber, Les Baer, Jerry Deane, Dopey Duncan, Joey Mitchell, Guy Randall Ackley, Bill Davis, Bob Grayson, Frank Todd, Edward The J, Double D, Ned Richards, Kerm Gregory, Don Bruce, Keith Reeth, Kevin Fennessey, Shotgun Steve Kelly, Mark Goodman, Cindy Drue, Bob Ross, Hopper Harvey, Ed Leonard, Jack Burns, Arnie Kriner, Ed Baumer, Jim Cameron, Dave Silverstein, Dave Fox, J Robert Taylor, Denny Somach, Chuck Henry, Dog Weldon and Jolly Joe Timmer were the guys that we heard on our radios daily. They were a big part of our lives. Whether they were counting down the top 40, doing live remote broadcasts or emceeing a high school sock hop, they were who we followed. And yes, we all had our favorites!

These were the guys who played the music, gave us the news, weather and sports. I remember Banana Nose Banaro(Tiger Joe McClaine) afternoons doing sports on WAEB. Alan Raber with the latest news and agriculture reports, Les Baer , Mickey Haggerty & Frantic Freddie with their oldies, Ernie Stiegler with "Toast & Coffee Time", " Sweet Soul,-Fast Talkin,- Sky King " Super Lou at night , Johnny Michaels broadcasting live from the HUB at the Allentown Y, Longtime morning man Bob Wolken with " This Day in History Segments ",The Babblin Brooke – Larry Brooke who used to talk a lot, Jolly Joe and his polkas, Bob Ross and his Underground Picks, Hopper Harvey flushing the toilet on the air, Steve Kelly with his Shotgun sounds and all the other various gimmicks that were used to liven up radio.

Those were the days of personality radio. They were fun, happy and unpredictable because you never knew what was coming next. Now, it is a long lost art form that we may never see again and it saddens me, because those days were memorable and left lasting impressions on everybody's lives. The shows were the best pieces of individuality ever heard. "Music for Lovers Only and Lovers Lonely" every Saturday Night, "American Top 40" with Casey Casem on Sunday, "The Friday Night Top 40 Count Down"

The legendary Jumpin' Jay Sands shown in this photo on his morning show in the late 60's on AM powerhouse WAEB which was then located at 700 Fenwick St in Allentown.

Jay was one of the original "WAEB good guys" at the station. Jay also emceed many dances, concerts and events in the Lehigh Valley area and appeared at local clubs with his oldies show. This was the DJ that the Lehigh Valley used to wake up to every morning from 6 AM until 9 AM.

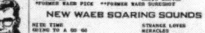

WSAN promo item of microphone and NBC's "Little Nipper"

WAEB RECORD SURVEY
Top Tunes in Lehigh Valley

No. 326 **RADIO 79**

Week of
OCTOBER 10, 1960

POS. THIS WEEK	SONG	ARTIST	LABEL	POS. LAST WEEK
1	The Twist	Chubby Checker	Parkway	1
2	My Heart Has A Mind Of Its Own *	Connie Francis	M-G-M	2
3	Mr. Custer	Larry Verne	Era	4
4	Let's Think About Livin' *	Bob Luman	WB	3
5	Theme From The Apartment	Ferrante & Teicher	UA	8
6	I Want To Be Wanted *	Brenda Lee	Decca	13
7	Chain Gang *	Sam Cooke	RCA-Victor	5
8	A Million to One *	Jimmy Charles	Promo	12
9	Anymore	Teresa Brewer	Coral	10
10	Devil Or Angel	Bobby Vee	Liberty	6
11	Save The Last Dance For Me *	Drifters	Atlantic	16
12	Lucille / So Sad	Everly Bros.	Warner Bros.	18
13	Togetherness	Frankie Avalon	Chancellor	11
14	Pineapple Princess *	Annette	Vista	7
15	Wait * / Come Back	Jimmy Clanton	Ace	14
16	Summer Is Gone	Paul Anka	ABC-Para.	20
17	Let's Have A Party	Wanda Jackson	Capitol	29
18	Hot Rod Lincoln	Charlie Ryan	Four Star	9
19	Twistin' U.S.A. *	Danny & Jrs.	Swan	15
20	Irresistible You	Bobby Peterson	V Tone	17
21	Artificial Flowers *	Bobby Darin	Atco	24
22	Run Samson Run	Neil Sedaka	RCA-Victor	21
23	Walk — Don't Run*	The Ventures	Dolton	25
24	Kiddio	Brook Benton	Mercury	31
25	Dreaming	Johnny Burnett	Liberty	22
26	Honest I Do	Innocents	Indigo	28
27	We Go Together	Jan & Dean	Dore	34
28	Don't Be Cruel	Bill Black's Combo	Hi	25
29	Peter Gunn	Duane Eddy	Jamie	—
30	In My Little Corner of the World *	Anita Bryant	Carlton	19
31	Volare *	Bobby Rydell	Cameo	26
32	It's Now Or Never	Elvis Presley	RCA-Victor	23
34	Cruel World *	Andy Starr	Veliant	36
36	I Never Knew	Dick Lee	Felsted	38
37	To Each His Own *	Platters	Mercury	—
38	Poetry In Motion *	Johnny Tillotson	Cadence	—
39	Shimmy, Shimmy *	Bobby Freeman	King	—
40	Count Every Star *	Tommy De Noble	Sheryl	39

*Former Big Six Pix of the Week (18)

The BIG Six Pix of the Week

JOE—Theme From The Sundowners—Felix Slatkin
BUD—The Magnificent Seven—Al Caiola
NEDD—One Of The Lucky Ones—Anita Bryant
ERNIE—The Story Of Jesse James—Jamie Coe
DON—The Hucklebuck—Chubby Checker
KERM—Two Little Monkeys—Revels

ALBUMS TO WATC

"For Teenagers Only"—Bobby Darin
"Italiannette"—Annette
"Ta Ta"—Clyde McPhatter

MUSIC
NEWS
SPORTS

HEAR WAEB'S NEWEST PERSONALITY
"DON BRUCE"
6:30 to 9:00 P.M.

YOUR GOO
NEIGHBOR STA
W A E B

A young Jack Burns on WSAN AM radio

184

Frantic Freddie WEEX

Bob Wolken WGPA

Jerry Deane WSAN

Rod Carson WAEB

Super Lou WAEB

Denny Somach WSAN

Guy Randall Ackley WAEB

Mark Goodman – WSAN

Bill Davis WAEB

Guy Randall Ackley WAEB

Mark Goodman – WSAN

Bill Davis WAEB

Jolly Joe Timmer – WGPA

Keith Reith – WHOL

Cousin Brucie – WABC

WABC – 77 billboard

WFIL Prize Patrol

John Lennon – RIP at WFIL

186

Old WSAN Microphone

WSAN Album Station T-Shirt

WKAP Oldies 1470

Gene Kaye/ The Crystals

Gene Kaye/ Herman's Hermit's

George Michael – WFIL

Dopey Duncan – WKAP

"The Geater" Jerry Blavat

Kevin Fennessy WKAP, WFIL

WGPA – Bethlehem, PA

WAEB Press Pass

Jack Burns – WALN

WEST Studios – Easton

WEEX Easton

60's style AM Studio

Les Baer WKAP & Tommy Zito

Joe Swanson WEZV/Z95 WSAN

Joey Alberts (RIP) WAEB

188

Famous 56 WFIL was one of the most listened to regional stations. Originating from City Line Ave in Philadelphia, The Boss Jocks entertained their audiences as well as broke new music before anyone else in the area. George Michael (RIP) went on to network and syndicated work with his show The George Michael Sports Machine before he passed. Dr Donald D Rose worked at quite a few major market stations in the country as well as the other jocks.

WFIL BOSS JOCKS - Dave Parks, Dr Donald D Rose, Long John Wade, Jim Nettleton, Jay Cook and George Michael – RIP

YOU'RE ALWAYS ON TOP

IN THE

WONDERFUL WORLD

OF

WIBBAGE

JERRY STEVENS
6 - 10 AM

ALLAN DEAN
2 AM - 6 AM

WIBG
Radio 99

BILL WRIGHT, SR.
10 AM - 2 PM

FRANK X. FELLER
10 PM - 2 AM

JOE NIAGARA
2 - 6 PM

HY LIT
6 - 10 PM

Philadelphia's Top Music Men

MORE people know that the WIBBAGE Good Guys KNOW their music. They're out front on the music scene . . . . fast and first with the hot releases, the new, exciting sounds . . . . no dead disks . . . . no "tired hits". Stay tuned to the wonderful world of WIBBAGE . . . . it's music to your ears.

PRACTICALLY EVERYBODY CALLS US BY OUR FIRST NAME—WIBBAGE

WIBG was another hot Philly station that Lehigh Valley people used to listen to in the 60's

CHAPTER 5: LEHIGH FM VALLEY RADIO

By the mid 1960's, cutting edge rock music responded by appearing on the newly created FM radio band, which was considered an "underground" means of airing music that favored longer songs, more controversial material and less restrictive programming styles. These DJ's began a revolution by eliminating the loudmouth hype between "Top 40" songs and adopting a cool, understated attitude, while playing music that previously never made it to the airwaves.

The mid 1960's witnessed the Vietnam War, political protests and racial riots that brought about social unrest, tumultuous times and extremely passive radio broadcasting. The counterculture revolution, the "children of the 60's" who later became the working class and yuppies of the 1970's, ultimately "killed" the movement (when the fringe culture became big business).

Regardless, this was an era of unknown bands and rare recordings of "far out" garage and psychedelic music. The years of 1965 through 1973 were the most experimental days of Rock and Roll, still reflected in today's music.

FM radio in the Lehigh Valley started to make some waves in the early 70's when stations that were playing beautiful music or what was referred to as "Elevator Music" started changing formats and inserting many different types of music. These stations could broadcast a quality signal in Stereo that was not yet available on the AM Bands and the sound was vastly superior. Top 40, Disco/Dance, Adult-Contemporary, Album-Oriented Rock, Underground and Oldies were the early mainstays of FM Radio.

The Lehigh Valley had quite a few FM Stations. WXKW –FM started as beautiful music, switched to country, moved to a Top 40 Format and then to a Hot Hits/Urban format under the guises of Laser 104.1 and B 104 under the calls of WAEB –FM. Ownership of the station has included Rust Communications, AM-FM and currently under Clear Channel.

WEEX – FM in Easton was originally playing beautiful music before switching formats and changing their calls to WHTZ Hot 99.9 playing an urban type Hot Hits/Dance Format. New ownership bought the station and changed the calls again to WQQQ. Q 100 and was a Hot Hits Format to give rival WAEB FM a go for their ratings share. After that failed experiment they changed ownership and calls again to WODE and started broadcasting oldies under the moniker of Oldies 99.9. They are now known as 99.9 The Hawk playing Classic Rock Standards and owned by Nassau Communications.

WGPA – FM was owned by the Globe Time Newspapers in Bethlehem and played beautiful music. They were sold to Holt Broadcasting and changed their calls to WEZV EZ-95 " The People in the Pyramid" They played a mixture of dance and Top 40 early on and then progressed to rock under the calls of WZZO Z-95 and moved the station to the Westgate Mall in Bethlehem. AM-FM/Clear Channel bought them and they are now in Whitehall, PA and are still doing that same AOR format today.

WEST-FM also played beautiful music and was sold and the calls were changed to WLEV FM 96 which played a more Adult-Contemporary format under the phrase "Best Mix, Most Variety ".They were sold by Citadel and are now WCTO, Cat Country 96. WFMZ –FM was also another station that played "Elevator Music" until the 90's when Maranantha sold them and they became 100.7 WLEV which carried the call and format to the new station.

Other FM'ers in the market are mainly low power college oriented such as WMUH at Muhlenberg College, WLVR at Lehigh University, WXLV and PBR affiliate WDIY in Bethlehem, PA.

Cable FM radio in the US started right here in the Lehigh Valley when Jack Burns approached Mr John Walson at Service Electric Cable with the idea of broadcasting live over the cable company's system. Mr Walson applied an received an FM frequency assignment and this was the start of cable FM in the U.S.

BRIEF 36 YEAR HISTORY OF WALN DIGITAL CABLE RADIO

WALN Digital Cable Radio in Salisbury Township was the Nation's First Commercial Cable Radio Station established in 1974.

From its humble beginnings in a 6 x 10 walk-in closet, WALN has grown from a few dozen local Cable FM subscribers to potentially millions of listeners and viewers worldwide!

WALN was founded by John J. Burnatowski also known as Jack Burns owner of the ABA Broadcasting Company.

In April of 1974, the late John Walson, Sr., the founder of cable television, granted a cable radio frequency of 92.1 MHz. on his FM system for WALN to offer programs to Service Electric Cable subscribers.

WALN signed on June 3, 1974 as the area's first rock and roll solid gold radio station. At the time there were no Lehigh Valley radio stations programming rock music on FM radio!

WALN continued that format until 1976, when it changed to Country Music.

Country music was featured on WALN until 1978, when the present Sentimental Hit Parade format was established.

In addition to music, WALN has provided the Lehigh Valley with Public Affairs, News and exclusive major league baseball and basketball coverage.

WALN received national recognition and awards over the years for outstanding programs.

In August of 1984, WALN began to deviate from the Sentimental Hit Parade music format on weekends and began the popular WALN Polka Weekend! Non-stop polka music all weekend long. This was unheard of in the history of polka music!

Today that tradition continues from 6 :00 Friday night through Sunday Midnight.

In 1995, WALN began to offer programs to Shortwave Radio listeners through WWCR in Nashville, TN.

In 2000, WALN began webcasting on the internet through WarpRadio in Colorado. WALN continues to stream audio 24/7 on the Internet!

In April of 2006, WALN switched from analog FM 92.1 to an all digital service available to Service Electric Digital Cable Subscribers throughout the Lehigh Valley, Northeastern PA and Western New Jersey.

In January, 2009, WALN began streaming live video on the internet through Livestream!

In December, 2009, WALN received recognition by John Walson, Jr, President of Service Electric Cable TV and Communications, for 35 years of Cable Radio and TV programming.

Today, WALN can be heard and viewed on Digital Channels 103 and 137 as well as walncableradio.com on the Internet. WALN is now known as The Party Channel.

The longest running program on WALN continues to be a Christmas holiday special called "The 12 Days of Christmas" which features holiday favorites from over 50 countries, worldwide. This program airing in December, 1974 continues every year on WALN and is the longest continuing radio program in the Lehigh Valley.

Happy Jack Burns in the studios of WALN in the 70's

Original WALN Broadcast Trailer in the 70's

Oldies 99.9 Casino Night – 1992 Mike Marder, Joey Mitchell(RIP) and Michael Anthony

WHXT HOT 99.9 Car Giveaway 1999 Check out this crew

Uncle Bob's Q -100 Limo

Q-100's Uncle Bob with Mario Andretti

L to R: Steve McNee (noon to 4PM shift), Gene Romano & Joan Edward-son (Morning Show team; Joan did the news, Tom "T.D." Kelly, 4PM-8PM shift & Program Director; Bruce Bond, 9:30am-noon, Music Director; SKIP Carr.

B -104's TNT Troy N Thomas

B 104's Ken Matthews

Brian McKay- Hot/Oldies 99.9

Todd Heft – WZZO, WODE   Bill Marvin – WLEV, WODE   Billy Sheridan, WKAP, WODE

Bearman, Tori Thomas & Keith – Z -95   Sting with Cindy Drue (WSAN & WMMR)

Blake Dannen WMMR & Z-95   Chris Line, Cat & Z-95   Laura St James – B 104

Kim Douglas & the Fonz   Phil Forchelli & Mike Fox Z95   Mike, Sam Kinison, Tony Jordan

198

WZZO Basketball Team is the WZZO staff in a team shot (early 80's) featured are Captain Mozzo, Gene Romano, Mark O'Brien, Steve McNee, Jim Loftus, T.D. Kelly, Cindy Holt

WZZO Staff and Def Leopard Soccer Teams – 1991 and 1999

WZZO Lightning Party Van   WZZO Birthday Cake

Cyndy Drue, Dick Hungate, Bill, former Journey vocalist Steve Perry, Lisa Richards, Denny Stomach, late CBS Records rep Herb Gordon at Philly's WYSP.

WYSP crew circa 1981 front: Joe Madden, Denny Stomach. 2nd: Dick Hungate, Cindy Drue, Patsy Althouse, Ed Anderson, Steve Feinstein, Dave Newman, R.D. Steele, Gil Bratcher

Ken Matthews B 104 Billboard on Route 22

CHAPTER 6: MUSIC TELEVISION

Television played an important part in music during the early days. There were many local and national outlets that presented live music in addition to their other act appearing on these shows. Cable television was also making inroads in local communities. We here in Allentown were fortunate to have the oldest and 1st cable company in the country with Service Electric Cable TV.

John Walson is regarded as the father of CATV(community antenna television). He was the first to offer the fledgling HBO Cable Channel a spot on Service Electric and the first original show that they broadcast was the Pennsylvania Polka Festival from the Allentown Fairgrounds. Twin County Cable located in East Allen Twp north of Allentown was the first to design a converter that allowed both play per view and regular analog cable channels in 1971. These companies were the first to be in direct competition in the same market in the US.

Presentations like The Ed Sullivan Show set the standard for live music appearing on TV from the late 50s on. But things changed drastically and ratings started to spike when rock & roll acts appeared live on TV. Locally produced shows started to appear pushing a music only format. Regional shows from the area included a music show called Kokomotion on WNEP 16 in Wilkes-Barre, The Ed Hurst Steel Pier Show live from Atlantic City NJ and a young DJ by the name Hy Lit who had local shows called "Hyski-A-Go-Go" and "The Hy Lit Show" on WKBS.

Hy Lit TV Show on WKBS 48 – Philadelphia

WNEP TV 16's Kokomotion

Ed Hurst's Steel Pier Show live from Atlantic City   Ed Hurst

The standard for all music shows was pioneered by Dick Clark who started a show named American Bandstand in 1957 on WFIL TV 6 in Philadelphia. This show became such a big hit that it went national on the ABC Network every Saturday afternoon. The eternal teenager was responsible for bringing mainstream rock & roll into the homes of people all across the US. His Rate-A-Record Segment, the Bandstand Dancers and New Song of the Week gave us a feel of how the everyday person reacted to today's sounds. He set the standard for other types of music shows to follow like Hullabaloo, Upbeat. Don Cornelius Soul Train & Don Kirshner's Rock Concert. Since there was no shortage of acts, bands and performers, every week was fresh and brought new music to the masses via television.

ick Clark, Fabian, Bobby Rydell and Frankie Avalon

Dick Clark & Bobby Rydell - 1958

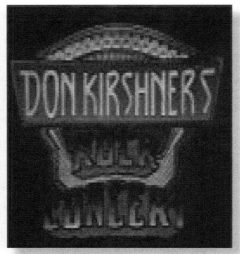

By the 80's, music on the tube evolved once again. Rock videos became the rage and cable TV was expanding channels to include all music channels. The pioneer in this new outlet was MTV – Music Television and later its sister channel VH-1 – Video Hits 1. MTV was launched on August 1, 1981 with the words "Ladies and gentlemen, Rock and Roll" spoken by John Lack The first video played on the air was entitled " Video Killed The Radio Star" by The Buggles and the first VJ or video-jock was Mark Goodman, previously employed by WSAN Radio 1470 in Allentown, Pa and WYSP in Philadelphia. The original five MTV VJs in 1981 were Nina Blackwood,

Mark Goodman, Alan Hunter, J.J. Jackson and Martha Quinn. SuperStation WTBS launched Night Tracks on June 3, 1983, with up to 14 hours of music video airplay each late night weekend by 1985. Its most noticeable difference was that black artists received airplay that MTV initially ignored. The program ran until the end of May 1992. Shortly after TBS began Night Tracks, NBC launched its music video program called Friday Night Videos which was considered network television's answer to MTV. Later renamed simply Friday Night, the program ran from 1983 to 2002, at which time it was replaced by other programming. ABC's contribution to the music video program genre in 1984, ABC Rocks, was far less successful, lasting only a year. VH1 launched on January 1, 1985 in the old space of Turner Broadcasting's short-lived Cable Music Channel, the original purpose of the channel was to build on the success of MTV by playing music videos, but targeting a slightly older demographic than its sister channel, focusing on the lighter, softer side of popular music.

Graphic by Joey P.

CHAPTER 7: THE EARLY TEEN & ADULT NIGHT CLUBS

The Lehigh Valley was the regional hotspot for clubs in the 60's & 70's. People used to come for miles around to see their favorite local bands and national acts that would perform on the stages in the area. Club owners and managers always tried to get the best acts for the weekends to attract the most people. They used all kinds of promotions like free T-Shirts, Ladies Nights, Battle of the Bands, Wet T Shirt Contests, Happy Hours, Dollar Drafts, College Nights and a host of others to attract customers. Sometimes they would have guest Emcees from local radio stations host the night's events or act as DJ's between bands.

Yours truly falls into that category. I got my start in my teens and worked into my late 40's as a club and radio DJ. It was a lot of fun and each night was a new challenge, especially working with bands. There were clubs that catered to teens only, rock clubs, folk clubs, country clubs, R&B clubs and nightspots with DJ's only. Every genre of music has been represented in the Lehigh Valley at one time or another.

Some of the early clubs were a mixture of teen and adult clubs. Some of the teen clubs included King Arthurs Court in Trainers, The Zoo and The Cameo in Allentown, The Mod Mill in Center Valley, The Mad Hatter and New Orleans Lounge in Allentown, Illick's Mill in Bethlehem, The Hub @ The YM/YWCA in Allentown, I Like It Like That, The Purple Owl in Allentown, Castle Rock in Dorneyville, Notre Dame Bandstand in Bethlehem and Saylor's Lake Pavilion.

KING ARTHUR'S COURT

King Arthur's Court was founded in 1967 by Mike Homick manager of the King's Ransom. Mike took a building which had previously been used for running model trains and turned it into a happening 60's night club for high school and college students between the ages of 16 and 21. Located one mile north of Quakertown, the court operated from 1967-1971 until the teen scene shifted to New Jersey prompted by the lower drinking age across the Delaware. Shrouded by thick green woods, King Arthur's Court frequently had two bands playing on the same night, one of which was usually the King's Ransom. Like the Mad Hatter and Mod Mill, the court had many national bands with hit records play there. Now an auto parts store, the building still looks very much as it did nearly 40 years ago, minus the sign of course.

THE PURPLE OWL/THE ZOO

The Purple Owl was the first of the late 60's teen clubs to open. Ken Bray got the idea watching the old TV show Hullaballoo which had popular bands playing every week. Success was the greatest problem Bray had to deal with, as neighbors did not take kindly to the thundering herd of teens that descended on the club many nights a week. The Purple Owl opened on December 29, 1966, and it was several months until the Mad Hatter, Mod Mill and King Arthur's Court came along to diminish the over-crowded conditions at the Owl. The West Coast Pop Art Experiment Band was one of the semi-national acts to play there along with local and regional acts. By the fall of 1967, Bray had enough visits from the police to no longer wish to continue his successful venture. The club re-opened under another owner as The Zoo on December 16, 1967. But the Zoo lasted for less than a year as well.

THE MAD HATTER

The Mad Hatter was located on Lehigh Street on the south side of Allentown, right next to McDonalds. It was regarded as the teen club to go to for great soul music. Operated by future concert promoter Tom Makoul, the Mad Hatter had many national acts perform their hits there, as well as the regular regional acts. R & B was the staple at the Mad Hatter, but local rock and garage bands played there also. The building still stands as pictured.

THE MOD MILL

The Mod Mill opened the same week in May of 1967 that King Arthur's Court began operating. You had to be 17 to attend Jerry Deane's establishment which he billed as a supper club for young adults. Deane, a well known Lehigh Valley DJ, seemed to want to present the Mill as a bit more upscale than the other teen discotheques in the area. The Mod Mill lasted only a couple years until it was forced to close by the state because of plans for highway expansion to route 309.

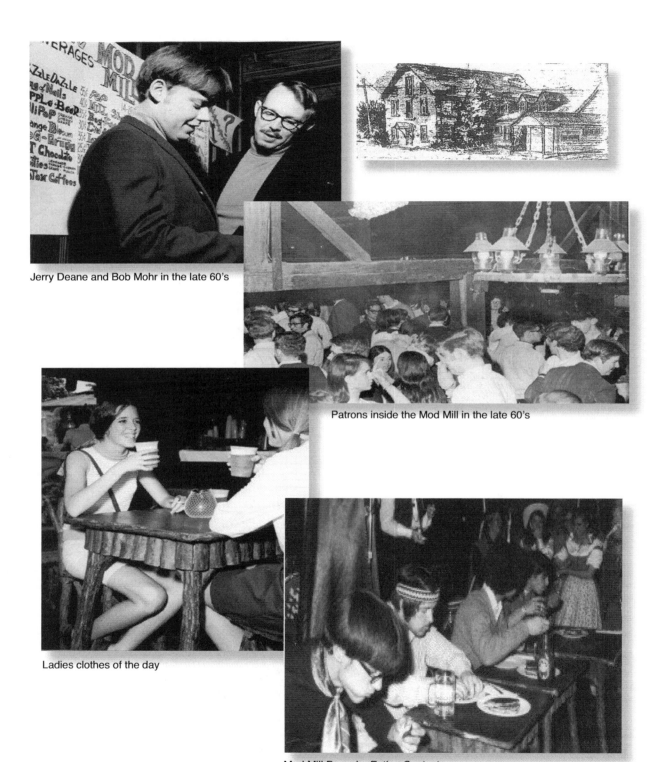

Jerry Deane and Bob Mohr in the late 60's

Patrons inside the Mod Mill in the late 60's

Ladies clothes of the day

Mod Mill Pancake Eating Contest

The Mod Mill

Private Club For Young Adults
Centre Valley, Pennsylvania

OPEN HOUSE — SUNDAY, NOVEMBER 30, 1969 — 12-5 P.M.

Erected 1774 — Demolished 1970

The Old Mill, originally built and operated as a grist mill nearly 200 years ago by Jacob Geissinger, was considered at that time the most modern mill in the east. Still intact are dual waterwheels and grindstones which could produce over twice as much flour as any mill in existence. Early in the 1900's, however, "Geissinger's Mill" began to feel the pressures of modern methods of milling and was forced to cease operations as a grist mill. Renovated at great expense, the old mill began serving as a rest for weary travelers along the "Old Philadelphia Pike" and offered 16 guest rooms, fine food, drinks and entertainment. The tales of "Old-Timers" tell of a booming business during the years of prohibition. In its later years, the old mill gained further fame as a rollicking nite-spot operated by the late Eddie Sachs, the renowned "Indianapolis 500" race car driver and featured a beloved old time piano player by the name of Charlie Young. In 1967 the mill came alive again as the Mod Mill — a modern concept of entertainment for young adults, a unique combination of modern music, modern people, modern thinking and cozy old English and Early American atmosphere. The Mod Mill, for almost 3 years has been a credit to the youth of our area having been operated almost entirely by the 1,000 members of the club. The only private club for young adults in a wide area it was attended by nearly 70,000 young people each year. Always maintaining the highest standards, the club was highly respected in the community and recognized nationally on many occasions. The management and the members have made plans to continue the services of the club in new facilities nearby but feel the loss of their "Old Mill Deeply." A landmark of early area history and a benchmark of social progress. The Mod Mill, Centre Valley, Pennsylvania.

Jerry Deano

Manager

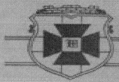

(The Mod Mill) a member of

Modern American Young Adult Clubs, Inc.

Distinguished Private Clubs for Young Adults

ILLICKS MILL

Before the Purple Owl opened late in 1966 there were a few places for bands to play other than high schools parties and fraternities. There had been a teen club in the mid 60's located in downtown Allentown called I like it like that. Then there was the Hub at the Allentown YMCA which had bands and in Bethlehem Illick's Mill is where it was all happening. An old stone farmhouse is w ere the teen club was located. Illick's Mill was known as the teen folk club featuring bands like The Munchkins on a weekly basis.

Illick's Mill today.

BILL DANIEL'S ROCK PALACE / MUSIC FACTORY

Located in Dorneyville on Hamilton Blvd (Old Rte 222) Bill Daniel's Rock Palace and its predecessor Caesar's Palace became the in place for rock bands to perform. Bill Daniel's, his wife Jenny and son John brought in local acts as well as regional acts that rocked the Lehigh Valley. A lot of movie stars and major national acts stopped there after their concerts to visit and experience the club. This list includes Billy Joel, Foreigner, Angel, Jayne Mansfield and Dianne Cannon. The club had gained national notoriety and was rated the #1 Rock Club in Eastern PA in 1976. In later years, it became the Music Factory which changed some and offered teens a place to go in the 80's.

Billy Joel, Ben Rose & Bill   The famous T-Shirt   Jenny Daniels

The Waitresses   Don Hunt, John & Bill Daniels   Lisa, John & Billy Daniels

John, Jenny & Bill Daniels with Tommy Zito and Magnum

Casablanca recording artists "Angel "and Bill Daniels

CASTLE GARDEN – DORNEY PARK

The ball room at Castle Garden has a great history. Starting with Big Bands in the 40's & 50's, The Garden offered a place for Lehigh Valley people to enjoy major acts. In the 60's, some of the country's hottest rock & roll bands played there when it was known as Castle Rock. The Garden was also used for High School Proms and graduation dances and some college events. Disco came to Castle Garden in 1978 after a major renovation that included the areas largest sound and light show. Roller Skating and Country Music followed in the later years until its demise.

Here are photos from around 1950 of an Allentown High School dance and table setup at Castle Garden in Dorney Park.

In Sept of 1978, a local club DJ by the name of Mike Jacobs (me) and with Bobby Plarr came up with an idea to broadcast live an entire evening of music commercial-free-at a local disco. At the time, the station was an independent local AM station. The PD, Chris Bailey, Station Mgr Jerry Duckett and the staff were very interested in the project that could help them in competition with their cross-town nemesis WAEB 790AM and add a possible ratings boost to the TOP40 outlet.

The facility to be used was "The Castle Garden Ballroom" located in Dorney Park in Allentown. The parks owners, Robert Plarr and Robert Ott were also on board for this project. After extensive renovations, Castle Garden was opened for business in the late fall of 78. Crowds averaged about 300-450 per night and the owners and mgmt were looking for a spark to drive this to bigger and better crowds. The ballroom had a capacity of approx 2000 people and 300-450 looked pretty thin at the time.

The idea was refined and in Jan of 79, Studio 13 debuted with a bang. It was broadcast Saturday's from 9:00 PM – 2:00 AM with DJ Mike Jacobs as the DJ/Host/MC. Bill Sheridan (now employed by Nassau Broadcasting) and Shotgun Steve Kelly were the board techs. Sponsorship for the show was secured and Pepsi-Cola came on board as the primary sponsor. Commercials were inserted by Bill & Steve by having Mike Jacobs back time the breaks in the music and then the station inserting voice-only commercials over the breaks in the music while the music played the instrumental break without interruption. The show opened with the Parliament's "Shit, Goddamn, Get Off Your Ass & Jam," followed by Bell & James' "Livin It Up". This resulted in an FCC Warning to the station and made the local news. The first night the crowd was 600 people. After the news coverage and word of mouth, Studio 13 averaged 2,000 people per night and could have done more had there not been a Fire Marshall's limit on the amount of people.

WKAP realized a ratings jump from 3.8 to 23.4, Saturday evenings from 9:00PM to 12 Midnight in a 1 month period and maintained this throughout the summer till the shows conclusion on Labor Day of 1979 at the park's request.

The management of Castle Garden also inve sted in and shot a 1-hour video pilot entitled "Castle Garden" that it attempted to syndicate. I was the music director for the pilot.

218

SAYLOR'S LAKE PAVILLION

Saylor's Lake Pavilion was the scene for many a gig by 60's and 70's bands both local and national in origin. Many famous names appeared at the Lake including The Devil's, The Dooley Invention, The Searchers, Tommy James & The Shondells, Borzoi, The 4 Seasons, Fanny, Brownsville Station, Cactus, Golden Earring, The Prophets, Dick and Dee Dee, The Dovells and Ronnie Dio (RIP). A lot of these gigs were produced by local DJ Gene Kaye.

THE GREEN PINE INN / CASEY'S

If you were a musician in the 1960s, 70s, 80s or 90s, you probably played at the Green Pine Inn located in south Allentown at one time or another. In the 1960s, the King's Ransom played there, as did the Limits. The Dooley Invention and D.B.L.I.T.Y played there in the 70s. In later years, Magnum, The Front, Gandalf, Witness and a host of others graced their stage. Never the gig you dreamed of for any given weekend. But for many years the Green Pine was a place to play and get paid for the effort. Many local and regional bands have played on their stage as well as many local DJ's in the booth. Clam and Jam nights were popular there also.

GODFREY DANIELS

Godfrey's has been around for a long while and has been the place where an aspiring songwriter, composer or lyricist can come and jam on Open Mike Nights. A lot of folk artists who made it big have shared the stage at Godfrey's Located in South Bethlehem it has been a favorite spot for the college crowd for years.

CHAPTER 8: ADULT CLUBS – MID 70'S TO PRESENT

There were many clubs for adults too! One of the most notable was Caesars Palace/Bill Daniels Rock Palace/The Music Factory in Dorneyville. Others were The Red Rooster in Alpha, NJ, Jamaican-A-GoGo/ Odysseus/ Scarlett O'Hara's in Bethlehem, The Green Pine Inn in Allentown, The Firehouse in Easton, The Lighthouse in Bethlehem, The Castle Inn in Philipsburg, NJ, The House of Webb in Trachsville, The Queen Victoria/Maple Grove, west of Allentown, Godfrey Daniels in Bethlehem, The Cameo in Allentown, The Dixon Street Saloon in Allentown. In later years other clubs like The Castle Inn in Phillipsburg, NJ, Hideaway Park, The Fun House , Club Dimensions/Lupo's & Mickey Kelley's in Bethlehem, Casey's, The Zodiac in Allentown, The Silo in Reading, Jon & Peters in New Hope and The Windsor House in Whitehall also hosted bands.

THE CAMEO

The Cameo was located in downtown Allentown near 6th and Union Streets. The Cameo in the early days was known for its popularity to showcase bands from the region and also bring in upcoming national acts to play their stage. Local acts such as The Dooley Invention and Slim Pickins and also national acts like Roy Buchanan have played there. The place always had a decent crowd and was well known throughout the area.

THE MAPLE GROVE

The Maple Grove was established as a night club by the owners of the Queen Vic who moved to be closer to Allentown. The new owners transformed the 200 year old stone building into more of a Rock Club which was better suited for local bands playing original material, like Shuffle (later known as Daddy Licks), D.B.L.I.T.Y. and Odyssey. The location was less than ideal (about 10 miles west of Allentown) and parking was hard to come by.

THE QUEEN VICTORIA

Country bars became popular in the 1970s and the Queen Vic was the best place to go to suck down a pitcher or two of your favorite draught and listen to country rock bands like Dusty Rose and Pickens Located on Snowdrift Rd, just west of Rt. 309 in Allentown, the Queen Victoria lives on in the memories of thousands who visited in its heyday and remember the good food that went along with the music.

THE RED ROOSTER

The Red Rooster, in Alpha, NJ, was the most popular club in the 1970s for Lehigh Valley high school and college students. It held about 200 people at one time and, unlike the teen clubs of the 60s, served alcohol. The building's dimensions were very similar to King Arthur's Court, however there was only one stage with one band playing on any given night. Business continued to be strong until the state reinstated 21 as the legal drinking age and not long after, the party for clubs like the Red Rooster was over. But in its heyday it was so crowded on weekends that people had to wait outside for others to leave the club in order to get in. Area acts such as Gandalf, Magnum, Pegasus, Fury, and regional acts like TT Quick have played there.

JOHN & PETERS' IN NEW HOPE

Opened in 1972, the club has showcased over 48,000 musicians and entertained over 640,000 guests since its inception. Some of the acts that have appeared there include: ODETTA • MARTIN MULL• LEON REDBONE • PENN & TELLER • CLARENCE GATEMOUTH BROWN • RICHIE COLE • JOHN SEBASTIAN • ERIC ANDERSON • GEORGE THOROGOOD • COUNTRY JOE MCDONALD • TEMPEST • NEW RIDERS OF THE PURPLE SAGE • JOHNNY'S DANCE BAND • MARIA MULDAUR • LOUDON WAINWRIGHT III • PAULA LOCKHART • ARTIE TRAUM • DAVID AMRAM • MICHAEL HURLEY • ROBERT HAZARD • MARY CHAPIN CARPENTER • STANLEY JORDAN • ROY BOOKBINDER • KENN

KWEDER • JULIE GOLD • FABULOUS HEAVYWEIGHTS • TOWNES VAN ZANDT • RICHIE SAMBORA• ROSALIE SORRELS • CHRIS EBERHARDT • JOHN HERALD • LUTHER GUITAR JR JOHNSON • GAMBLE ROGERS • JOHN HAMMOND • JIMMY FAST FINGERS DAWKIN • HOLMES BROTHERS • SHAWN PHILLIPS • RORY BLOCK • JONATHAN EDWARDS • BUZZY LINHART • JAMIE BROCKETT • SAUL BRODY • THE FLAMIN' CAUCASIANS • NORAH JONES • DUKE WILLIAMS& THE EXTREMES • LIVINGSTON TAYLOR • WEEN • FRANK STALLONE VALENTINE • AZTEC TWO STEP • THE CHAMBER BROTHERS • MOUNTAIN JOHN • NIGHTHAWKS • MICHAEL HURLEY • CLIFTON CHENIER • ELLEN MCILWAINE • SAFFIRE • ESSRA MOHAWK • NEW ST. GEORGE • CHRIS SMITHERS • REILLY & MALONEY • BLUESMAN WILLIE • CHAD MITCHELL • JOHN GORKA • BLUE SPARKS FROM HELL • QUEEN BEE & THE BLUE HORNETS • FLAMIN HARRY • EDDIE SHAW • TERRANCE SIMION & THE MALLET PLAYBOYS • PHOEBE LEGERE • JOHN HERALD • IRON BUTTERFLY • DAVID MASSINGILL • STEVE FORBERT • TONY BIRD • BADFINGER • ORLEANS • DANNY KALB • BRYAN BOWERS • VASSAR CLEMENTS • SHAWN PHILLIPS • TINY TIM • SLIM PICKINS •

THE OLD LEHIGH TAVERN / FUNHOUSE

Once known as The Lehigh Tavern, The Funhouse has been entertaining crowds for about 25 years. Known as the place "where fun people meet & party", The Funhouse has carried on the traditions set down by The Lehigh Tavern since its inception. Bands and performers are the staple there for the college crowd and they include many different genres of music, but mainly present rock, alternative and folk/rock acts.

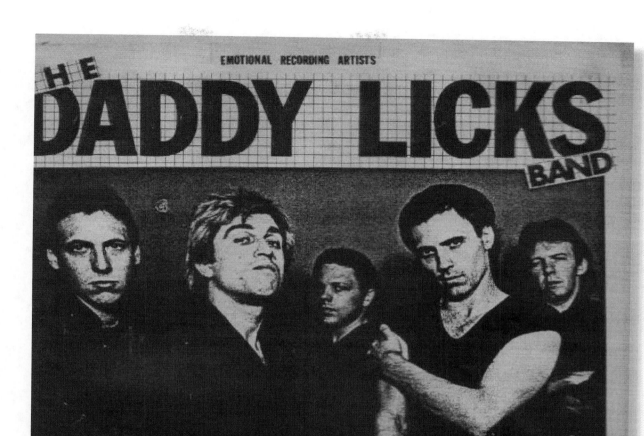

EMOTIONAL RECORDING ARTISTS

THE DADDY LICKS BAND

ROCKS

THE SPRINGHOUSE TAVERN

EVERY WEDNESDAY

CLUB PASCAL The All-Night Nite Spot 433-6788

A Music Club run by the Pennsylvania Association of Songwriters

Located in the Rear of the Airport Bingo. IN MART PLAZA. Airport Road, Allentown

The Lehigh Valley's *Only* Club Featuring
Live Entertainment Every Weekend
12 Midnight till 5 A.M.

Come out and Party all Nite long to the hottest acts from Philadelphia, New York and the Lehigh Valley. D.J.s spin the best in recorded music between sets.

ADMISSION $4.00 Members
$5.00 Non - Members

B.Y.O.B. You Must Be 21 to Enter

Bring your own bottle. Ice, Mixers & Cups Availa
Our Kitchen serves a Full Menu (Pizza, Steak
B.B.Q. Shrimp Salad and much more!) till 5 A
Come see for yourself, What everyones talking ab

Every Saturday 7 - 11 P.M.
Rock & Roll for ALL AGES
"A SUPER DANCE PARTY FOR EVERYONE"

Thursday Nights 9 to 2 A
NEW TALENT NIGHT
College Radio Station

THE HOUSE OF WEBB
PRESENTS IN APRIL, MAY, JUNE

APRIL		
	16-18-19	—MAGNUM
	23-25-26	—STEPH
APRIL		
	30(WED. NITE ROCK SPECIAL)	ERICK
MAY		
	2-3	SLANDER
	7-9-10	ERICK(House favorite)
	14-16-17	GANDALF
	21-23-24	STEPH
	28-30-31	RASPUTIN
JUNE		
	4-6-7	GOLDILOCKS
	11-13-14	ERICK
	18-20-21	STEPH
	25-27-28	BINGO'S DIE

KITCHEN OPEN———MON. THRU SAT.

SPECIALIZING IN SEAFOOD, STEAKS, CHOPS.

BANQUETS FROM 25-500

#1 ROCK CLUB IN THE POCONOS

Fluxstuff BAR ROOM & RESTAURANT

Friday January 11, 10 P.M.
LIVING EARTH
In Concert
GRATEFUL DEAD SHOW
No Admission Charge

ON TOP OF THE WORLD
Between Lehighton & Jim Thorpe (Rt. 209)
717-325-4554

From L.A. **THE DESCENDENTS**
THE GUNS
THE VIPERS
THE CREATURES

DJ BANANAS
992 3rd St., Whitehall 261-0600

TONIGHT
THE ARMADILLOS
with guest BIG FISH LITTLE POND
(featuring Scott Hof)

NO COVER BEFORE 9 P.M.
With this ad)

Mon. — GANDALF
Feb. 17 — BLACK OAK ARKANSAS

Rock 'n Roll
Tonight
DR. LOVE & THE JOINTS JUMPIN

PINE INN

COMEDY TONIGHT
George Sharp
Chuck Cornelius

Show Starts at 10:30

CHAPTER 9: THE ART OF DISCO IN THE 70'S

In the mid 70's Disco music made its mark on the Lehigh Valley. A plethora of dance clubs burst onto the scene in quick order. These were low budget clubs that had a sound and light system only for DJ's to play their music. Some of these clubs had DJ's and bands nightly. The clubs and discos include Bill's Apartment/ Bill Daniels's Rock Palace in Allentown, The Stonewall in Allentown, The Phase V in Bethlehem, The Oar House in Allentown, Odysseus in Bethlehem, Castle Garden at Dorney Park, The Wardell in Phillipsburg, PA, Second Time Around in Easton, Larry Holmes Round One in Easton, The Club, The Green Pine Inn, Main Gate, Dukes Pub, Club Dimension, Jetport and Alexander's in Allentown just to name a few. DJ's like myself, Mike Jacobs, Jimmy Chennault, Jamie Harter, Crankin' Ank Stimpfl, Tony C, Don Hunt, Jerry Deane, Vince Palau, " Mad Dog Fagan" Jimmy Krupa, Tom Price, Billy South, Debbie Makai, Chris Baraket, Freddie Frederick, Joey Mitchell, TNT, and Dave Encarnacion (RIP) just to name a few made their marks as club DJ's in these clubs. Here are the top disco songs of the era.

1. Don't Leave Me This Way--(Thelma Houston)
2. I Will Survive--(Gloria Gaynor)
3. You Make Me Feel Mighty Real-- (Sylvester)
4. Dance, Dance Dance--(Chic) 5.Disco Inferno--(Trammps)
6. Please Don't Let Me Be Misunderstood--(Santa Esmeralda)
7. Turn The Beat Around--(Vicki Sue Robinson)
8. Love To Love You Baby--(Donna Summer)
9. Fly Robin Fly--(Silver Convention)
10. I Love the Nightlife--(Alicia Bridges)
11. Shake Your Booty--(KC & The Sunshine Band)
12. Get Dancin'--(Disco Tex and the Sex-O-Lettes)
13. Disco Nights (Rock Freak)--(GQ)

MAINGATE
NIGHT CLUB

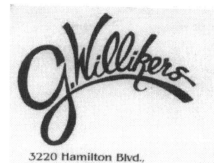

G.Willikers

Food, Spirits
& Dancing

3220 Hamilton Blvd.,
Allentown, PA 18103

Owners
Bill & Gen Daniels
437-9961

DJ CHRIS BARAKET
SATURDAYS

STONEWALL
MOOSE LOUNGE BAR & GRILLE

MUSIC FACTORY

TUXEDO
JUNCTION

DJ Don Hunt – RIP Rock Palace

DJ Jim Chenault – Stonewall & PJ Tiffany's

DJ JJ Sands – Main Gate & Roosevelts

DJ Randall C , Casey's, Green Pines

DJ TNT – Troy N Thomas – Main Gate 80's

DJ Crankin Ank Stimpfl – Dukes

DJ Freddie Frederick Jr.

DJ Dan Kocher

DJ Tony Casciano

DJ Jerry Deane – Rock Palace & Phase 5

DJ Mike Zweifel

Charicature of Michael Jacobs McKenna

DJ Mike Jacobs (me) - Rock Palace/Music Factory, Castle Garden/Studio 13 WKAP, Main Gate/ Sports Gate, Odysseus/Scarlett O Hara's, Club PASCAL, B & G Station, Hideaway Park, The Wardell.

CHAPTER 10: LEHIGH VALLEY CONCERTS

Where do I start here? Concerts were a mainstay in the Lehigh Valley for many years. From the 60's to the end of the century many different venues have been used to host national acts. I can remember seeing shows at many different places and all of them left lasting memories, some good, some not so good. The Lehigh Valley with its natural location between New York and Philadelphia was a natural spot for act to come to during their tours. Many a sold out show was performed here and quite a few recordings and videos were made here in later years. Some of the promoters who took the leap and gave the Valley memories include Dave Sestak with his Extensions of Man/Media 5 Productions, Jerry Deane with Mayac Productions, Tom Makoul of Makoul Productions, DeCaesar/Engler Productions, Electric Factory, WSAN/Roxy Theater, Mike Jacobs Entertainment, PASCAL, Sam Younes, The Allentown Council Of Youth, Musikfest & The Allentown Fair

The venues range from big grandstands to clubs. These include colleges like NCCC, LCCC, Kutztown, Lehigh, Muhlenberg and Moravian. Clubs like The Cameo, Mad Hatter, Mod Mill, used to host national acts in the 60's. Notre Dame High School and Saylor's Lake Pavilion were also big 60's concert spots. Agricultural Hall and The Grandstand at The Allentown Fairgrounds hosted some of the bigger shows in the 60's & 70's. Outdoor concerts gained strength in the 70's with shows being held at The Fairgrounds, Lehigh Parkway. & the Union Terrace. In later year's concert venues such as Stabler Arena, The Airport Music Hall and Symphony Hall presented shows from national acts. Clubs like Hideaway Park, Club PASCAL, The Zodiac, Club Dimension/Lupos and The Green Pine Inn also did some national acts.

During the 80's, The Allentown Council of Youth, PASCAL, smaller promoters and local radio stations presented outdoor concerts in Lehigh Parkway, Cedar Beach, Union Terrace, Kuhn's Grove, Cementon Playground and Evergreen Lake with a mixture of local and regional acts.

The Allentown Fair was the major concert place to be at the end of each summer when such national acts as Englebert Humperdink, Chicago, Tom Jones, Kansas, The Supremes, The Osmond's, Johnny Cash, Olivia Newton John, Rod Stewart, Alabama, Willie Nelson, Crosby, Stills & Nash, The Beach Boys, Lynyrd Skynyrd, Foreigner, James Taylor, Roy Rodgers, Andy Williams, Herb Alpert and a host of others played at the grandstand.

Concerts were also being held at The Roxy Theater in Northampton. Artists such as Bruce Springsteen, Billy Joel, Blood, Sweat & tears, Fleetwood Mac, Martin Mull, The Sensational Alex Harvey band, Gilda Radnor, Golden Earring, Kiss and Melissa Manchester were among those who performed in the concert series hosted by progressive rock outlet WSAN.

Area colleges like Muhlenberg, Lafayette, Moravian, Kutztown, LCCC & NCCC have seen such shows as ELO, The Romantics, Joan Jett & The Blackhearts, Willie Nelson, Procol Harem, Aerosmith, Dave Mason, Manfred Mann's Earth Band, Rick Wakeman, The Fifth Dimension, Frank Zappa, Leon Redbone and The New York Dolls.

Smaller venues like Agricultural Hall hosted shows like Sly & the Family Stone, Steam, The Flaming Embers and a host of others. Symphony Hall was another local site used for shows. Resorts like Saylor's Lake Pavilion were also a concert and local band mainstay. The shows ranged from oldies to rock and included Cactus, Brownsville Station, Fanny, Jay & The Techniques, The Searchers, The Dovells, The Prophets, Dick & Dee Dee and Ronnie James Dio.

Local DJ Gene Kaye also was a concert promoter and used a high school for his Notre Dame bandstand which features top name acts of the day including The Herman's Hermits, The Crystals and The Coasters. Promoters such as Jerry Deane and his Mayac Productions and Dave Sestak and the Extensions of Man Concerts made their marks in the 70's promoting shows in the area.

Staber Arena on the campus of Lehigh University became the largest indoor venue in the Valley and shows became the staple there also. Acts such as Nirvana, Whitney Houston, Bad Company, Marc Anthony, Bob Dylan, Bad Yankees, Poison. The Del Vikings, The Vogues, Grass Roots, Herman's Hermits, Danny & The Juniors, Bill Haley's Comets, The Del Vikings have also played there for The Christmas Spectacular Shows over the years.

In Bethlehem, in 1984 a group called ArtsQuest came up with an idea for a regional music festival. It started small but has grown to one of the largest in the US since its inception. With the emphasis on all genres of music and free shows, it became the place to be for artists and performers each August. Past headlining shows have included Stone Temple Pilots, Clay Aiken, Air Supply, Alice in Chains, Boston, The Beach Boys, Tony Bennett, Boyz II Men, Collective Soul, Ray Charles, George Clinton, Dixie Chicks, Dr. Demento and Weird Al Yankovic, Poison, Duran Duran, Earth, Wind & Fire, Fuel, Ludacris, Hootie & the Blowfish, Kool & The Gang, Jethro Tull, Jonny Lang, Lynyrd Skynyrd, Martina McBride, Steve Miller Band, Live, REO Speedwagon, Staind and George Thorogood.

Local German roots are the foundation of the celebration, and most of the festival's venues use the German word for place, "platz", at the ends of their names. A popular place for eating and listening to music, for example, is the large "Festplatz", which includes 300 dining tables and usually features a polka band each night. Beyond that, however, Musikfest's music, food and other attractions represent a broad range of ethnicities.

In Allentown, another festival, called Mayfair debuted in 1987 and was mainly arts, crafts and some music. This has grown into a 5 Day Festival of the Arts and is now the premier spring festival in the region on Memorial Day Weekend. The festival has grown and now has many stages for performances by live acts and lots of space for craft and art vendors. Many different national and local – regional acts have performed there.

STABLER ARENA

Stabler Arena is Lehigh University's 6,000-seat multi-purpose arena in Bethlehem, PA and is located on its Goodman Campus in the Lehigh Valley region of Pennsylvania. Opened in 1979, Stabler is an all-purpose arena, hosting athletic events, major concerts, car shows and children's events. Promoters like Tom Makoul of Makoul Productions, Larry Magid of Electric Factory Concerts, John Scher and others promoted shows there for years on a regular basis. Some of the major acts that appeared there include Atlanta Rhythm Section, Whitney Houston, Bad Company, Billy Joel, Hall & Oates, Bad Yankees, Ozzy Osbourne, the Herman's Hermits, Grass Roots, Tommy James and The Shondells, Nirvana, Bryan Adams, Aerosmith, Bob Dylan, Fleetwood Mac, Grateful Dead, Yes, Scorpions, David Lee Roth, David Gilmour from Pink Floyd, Poison & Metallica, Alvin Lee & Mick Taylor, Peter Gabriel,

The grunge rock band Nirvana performed at Stabler on November 9, 1993, less than five months before lead singer Kurt Cobain committed suicide at his Lake Washington residence. This show has since become one of the band's most widely circulated bootleg recordings because of its proximity to Cobain's death, representing one of Nirvana's final U.S. shows

Some bands have kicked off their tours at Stabler and they include The Cranberries, Kiss, Bette Midler and The Moody Blues.

On October 1, 1992, the rock band Kiss kicked off their global tour at Stabler Arena. Kiss's Stabler concert was the first arena show on the tour, following smaller, warm-up venues in Europe and the U.S. It was the first show to use a giant, pyrotechnic mock up of the Statue of Liberty

DJ Mike Jacobs (me) - Rock Palace/Music Factory, Castle Garden/Studio 13 WKAP, Main Gate/ Sports Gate, Odysseus/Scarlett O Hara's, Club PASCAL, B & G Station, Hideaway Park, The Wardell.

Pink Floyd - July12, 1984 Stabler Arena, live broadcast!

Alvin Lee at Stabler Arena

237

ELVIS COSTELLO & The Attractions

BETHLEHEM, PA

April 12, 1979

ADMIT ONE   THIS DATE
FEB 5 1981

JOHN SCHER
LEHIGH U SAC
PRESENT
GERRY GARCIA
BAND
* * *
STABLER ARENA
LEHIGH UNIV.
FEB 5 1981
THU 7:30 PM

NO REFUNDS PRICE NO EXCHANGES
$8.50

SEC   ROW   SEAT
21   J   8
CONCOURSE

Darryl Hall & John Oates live at Stabler Arena

AGRICULTURAL HALL

AG Hall as its known locally was one of the mainstays of the concert scene in the late 60's and early 70's due to the lack of other indoor sites in the Lehigh Valley. Located on the grounds of the Allentown Fair in the west end of Allentown, Ag Hall served up some unique and memorable shows such as Rush, Sly and the Family Stone, Steam, Flaming Ember, Mott the Hoople, Stone Temple Pilots, Megadeath, Billy Joel, Montrose, Budgie, Angel and AC DC.

Montrose at Ag Hall - 1970

Marshall Tucker Band - 1978

Steam, Flaming Ember - 1970

Budgie at Ag Hall 1970

Sly & the Family Stone at Ag Hall 1970

Billy Joel in dressing room

NOTRE DAME BANDSTAND

Notre Dame Bandstand was located in the High School Gym in Bethlehem, PA. Local radio DJ Gene Kaye (Kolber), as he was known on Allentown's WAEB during the '60s, hosted a Top 40 radio show, threw dance parties for teenagers around the Lehigh Valley like "Notre Dame Bandstand"--a record hop with notable guests that drew thousands--and discovered and managed a few music groups. Gene would bring the day's hottest acts to perform for the teen crowd. The bandstand became a very popular stop for bands looking to get exposure for their music and the band. Some of the bands that performed there were The Crystals, Herman's Hermits, The Dovells, Jay & The Techniques, The Cyrkle, Beau Brummels, The Toys, The Orlons, Brian Hyland, The Crests, The Searchers and local acts like the Union of Sound.

Teens dancing at Notre Dame Bandstand

Gene Kay with
Heman's Hermits

Heman's Hermits

Gene Kaye & the Crystals

241

MUHLENBERG COLLEGE

Muhlenberg College's Memorial Hall has been the scene of many great shows from the 60's to the 90's. All genres of music from Rock to Jazz to R&B to Alternative and Top 40 have been across the stages there. I remember seeing Marilyn McCoo, Billy Davis Jr. and The Fifth Dimension there on their Aquarius tour. Other notables that have played there include Bob Dylan, Traffic, The Kinks, The Romantics, Single Bullet Theory, Cat Stevens, The Psychedelic Furs, Black Oak Arkansas, The Turtles, Bruce Springsteen and a host of others.

Marilyn McCoo, Billy Davis Jr. and the Fifth Dimension – Aquarius Tour

Traffic played with Cat Stevens in 1972

Wow, look at the ticket price - $4 advance

242

Frank Zappa smoking a cigarette and signing autographs after a Mothers of Invention concert at Muhlenberg College on or about April 26, 1969. The headliners were the Turtles, who went on first. Nearly everyone left when the Mothers of Invention hit the stage. After the concert I took this photo and the few remaining teenaged hardcore Zappa fans (and their girlfriends) started

The Kinks - Muhlenberg College, Allentown, PA - 1981 - Another night where you see a band that's simply "on". People were on their feet for nearly the entire show. Even Ray Davies seemed surprised by the crowd reaction when he thanked us at the end of the show.

The Kinks - Muhlenberg College, Allentown, PA - 1981 - Another night where you see a band that's simply "on". People were on their feet for nearly the entire show. Even Ray Davies seemed surprised by the crowd reaction when he thanked us at the end of the show.

The Romantics, Single Bullet Theory & Crisis played at Memorial Hall in March of 1983. Mike Jacobs Entertainment (me) produced this show. It was my 1st major production.

NCCC - NORTHAMPTON COUNTY COMMUNITY COLLEGE

NCCC was the scene of many concerts that were promoted by Dave Sestak of Media 5 Entertainment and Extensions of Man Concerts. Back in the late 60's and early 70's some of rock music's major acts played there. Such acts as a young Billy Joel, ELO - The Electric Light Orchestra

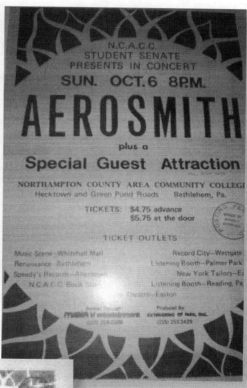

THE ALLENTOWN FAIRGROUNDS

The Allentown Fairgrounds has been the scene of many shows of all genres of music going back to its inception in the early 1900's. Yearly, the week before Labor Day, The Great Allentown Fair hosts grandstand show featuring some of the best acts from around the world.

Englebert Humperdink, Chicago, Tom Jones, Kansas, The Supremes, The Osmond's, Johnny Cash, Olivia Newton John, Rod Stewart, Alabama, Willie Nelson, Crosby, Stills & Nash, The Beach Boys, Lynyrd Skynyrd, Foreigner, James Taylor, Roy Rodgers, Andy Williams, Herb Alpert and a host of others played at the grandstand during the fair.

Local promoters like Makoul Productions also used the grandstand during the summer months to bring major recording acts to Allentown. Supertramp, Jan Hammer Group, Jeff Beck, UFO, Moxie, Montrose, Budgie, ZZ Top, Styx, The Allman Brothers, Stevie Ray Vaughn, Bryan Adams, Hootie & The Blowfish, Motley Crue, Foghat, Johnny Winter, Molly Hatchett & Little River Band are a few that come to mind. There are so many others that I could list that it would fill many pages.

Molly Hatchet at the Fairgrounds - 1979

ZZ Top at the Allentown Fair

Yes ticket stub from 1994

Ritchie Blackmore – 1970

246

Foghat - 1978

Twisted Sister and Ratt – 1984

247

Supertramp at the Fairgrounds June 19, 1976

Rush at the Fairgrounds 1983

AIRPORT MUSIC HALL

The Airport Music Hall was founded in 1984 as a place where performers could play their original music. The brainchild of The Pennsylvania Association of Songwriters, Composers and Lyricists (PASCAL) and its President John Havassy, the Music Hall became the spot to be to see great shows. Located inside an old supermarket, the Hall could hold about 1000 people for all age shows. BYOB was allowed in the balcony area in a strictly controlled atmosphere. In the early years, there were quite a few original local acts that played and got their start there and in its sister club in the back, Club PASCAL, which could hold about 150 patrons. I was deeply involved here as A VP/Secretary of PASCAL and a member of the Board of Directors until 1990.

There were some notable events that happened there. Guns N Roses played there as an opener 3 weeks before their LP was released for the Japanese hard rock band EZO. Chick Corea and his band Return to Forever used the Music Hall for a week to practice their show for their upcoming World Tour and gave the Music Hall a free show for the use of the hall as they opened their tour there.

Notable performers who have graced the stage there include Johnny Winter, Joan Jett, Expose, Pretty Poison, Flamin Harry's Blues Band, Leslie West from Mountain, Mark "The Animal" Mendoza from Twisted Sister, Level 42, Robert Hazard, UFO, Savatage, TT Quick, Heaven's Edge, Dirty Looks, The Rollins Band with Henry Rollins from Black Flag, The Cro Mags, Pantera, Prophet, Bad English, Treason, Fractured Seconds, The Mighty Bosstones, Wratchild America, The A's, Britney Fox, Saxon, Macauley-Schenker Group, Yngwie Malmsteen, The Del Fuegos, Phantom, Rocker & Slick, The Ramones and others.

Local and regional acts who also played the stage and made waves in the Valley include Destroyer, Washed, White Hott, Teeze, Mucky Pup, St John's Alliance, Crisis, Daddy Licks, Steve Brosky, Dave Fry, The Blessing, Kraken, Leviathan, The Trendsetters, The Descendants, Vicious Barreka, Sorcerer, Sapient, Sweet Tequila, Agnostic Front, Big Fish Little Pond, Howe II, Murphy's Law, The Dead End Kids, Zebra, Metalwolf, Babyface, The Rebeltones and Joey Saint.

The Music Hall lasted about 7 ½ years before they lost their lease and it left a big void in the area for mid-level acts and venues that could host shows for 1000 people. Sadly, there is nothing around today that matches it and only Crocodile Rock, Penn's Peak, The Allentown Fair and the regions music festivals come close to offering some semi-national and national acts in the area.

My memories of the Music Hall and the performers and band members that I met will always be with me. I am still friends with quite a few of them today still and we do communicate often. The patrons of the Music Hall were some of the best party people that I have ever met and many still keep in contact with me. Here are some of those good memories!

Chick Corea

Level 42

Leslie West & Mark Mendoza

Joan Jett

Yngwie Malmsteen

UFO

Robert Hazard

Dirty Looks

Bad English

250

The Mighty BossTones

Wrathchild America

Britny Fox

Teeze

The A's

Earl Slick,"Slim Jim" Phantom and Lee Rocker

The Del Fuegos

T T Quick

The Ramones

The Heartbeats

Exposé

Crisis

252

Kraken

The Blessing

St. John's Alliance

Leviathan

Vicious Barreka

Sapient

Sorcerer

Destroyer

Nasty Nasty

Washed

Joey Saint

Fractured Seconds

254

The Rebeltones

White Hott

Big Fish Little Pond - 1989

The Flamin' Harry Band

THE ROXY THEATER

By June 1st, 1970 when the theatre was acquired by Angstadt and Wolfe Theatres, it was only a shadow of its former glory. A&W began a slow and long drawn-out restoration of the theatre that still continues to this day. They also reintroduced live entertainment in the form of concerts, plays, magic shows and weddings. Artists such as Bruce Springsteen, Billy Joel, John Belushi, Blood, Sweat & Tears, The Sensational Alex Harvey Band, Kiss, Golden Earring and many others were featured under the sponsorship of radio station WSAN. The WSAN concert series brought many national and upcoming entertainers to the Lehigh valley area. The stations format, which was progressive underground rock, seemed to fit the day and the artists who would appear at The Roxy Theater.

Collage of artists that appeared at The Roxy on display in lobby

Collage of artists that appeared at The Roxy on display in lobby

Bruce Springsteen

UFO

John Martyn

Music To Be Soulful With

SEPT. 29

6:30 & 9:30 PM

FUZZY BUNNY

and TRUST

DOOR PRIZES

at the Roxy theatre
2004 Main St., Northampton, Pa.
benefit for Folly & Lehigh Valley Child Care
Tickets $2.50 - $3.00 at the door

Tickets on sale now at:
New York Tailors, Easton · Phantasmagoria, Allentown
Listening Booth, Palmer Park Mall · Speedy's, Allentown
Music Scene, Whitehall Mall · Renaissance, Bethlehem
Record City, Westgate Mall · Rock N' Roll Heaven, Bethlehem
WSAN Radio · Negro Cultural Center, Allentown
or by mail from Folly; Box 1061, Bethlehem, Pa. 18018
A Free Flowing Creative Forces Production

Two great area bands!

260

Cactus

Rick Danko poster

Hall and Oates

Golden Earring

Leo Sayer

Little Feat

Livingston Taylor

Nils Lofgren

Mahavishnu Orchestra

Peter Frampton

Status Quo

Steeleye Span

Climax Blues Band

David Bromberg

OTHER VENUES & SHOWS

Nazareth played at the Fairgrounds in 1974 and The Nazareth Speedway in 1978

The Turtles, played the Christmas Spectacular – Camelot for Children at Stabler Arena

Crack The Sky played with Rush at The Astor Theater in Reading 1976

NY Rock & Roll Ensemble played Grace Hall @ Lehigh in the 60's

Blue Oyster Cult at the Zodiac Club

Peter Noone from the Herman's Hermits at the Camelot for Children
Christmas Show at Stabler

Jean Luc Ponty - Played @ Symphony Hall, Allentown in 1977 on the Enigmatic Ocean Tour

Marshall Tucker Band - played Allentown in 1978

Doc Holliday at Hideaway Park in Bethlehem

Rush at the Astor Theater in Reading with Crack The Sky – 1976

OUTDOOR CONCERTS

This is a live shot taken at the Harrisburg Rock Festival in 1972, Joe Ziegenfuss on trombone, Steve Mamay on guitar, and Bobby Scammell on bass.

Ormai's Farm - Concert in 1971

Steppin Out at Union Terrace in Allentown, PA. In this photo: Christopher Jones, Reid Tre Dave Fry Dennis Danko

Rasputin live @ Lafayette College In this photo: Gregory Roth Bill Cobel

John Havassy & Mike McKenna in our PASCAL trailer backstage @ The Allentown Fair

Daddy Licks Concert, Dave Goddess – Lehigh Parkway

Blue Plate Special in the Lehigh Parkway

The Bandstand - 1984 Lehigh Parkway

Crowd at Lehigh Parkway in late 60's

CHAPTER 11: THE LOCAL SCENE FROM DAYS LONG GONE

The local scene in the 60's and 70's was dominated by the downtown areas of the 3 big cities of the Lehigh Valley, Allentown, Bethlehem and Easton. People used to congregate on the main drags downtown such as Hamilton Street during the evening hours to cruise the downtown or go to the theaters. Guys looking for chicks, chicks looking for guys, motor heads spinning their wheels with their muscle cars or hot rods and everyone listening to their tunes on the radio or their 8 - track or cassette tapes. The Ritz Barbeque was the big hangout spot and at any given time on weekends there was upwards of 200 cars in the lot with people just hanging out having fun. Once in a while, you could catch a good drag race on the ¼ mile behind the ASD Stadium.

On Sundays, the place to be was the Lehigh Parkway. People used to cruise thru the Parkway from about Noon until dusk and be able to park on both sides of the road. On any given Sunday, bikes, muscle cars, family station wagons, party vans numbered in the hundreds. People roamed the park with their Frisbees, went fishing, had cookouts, listened to music or just looked at the procession of vehicles that used to come thru the Parkway all afternoon. Certain parts of the Lehigh Parkway were home to different segments of people. Robin Hood was the hippie hangout. The Iron Bridge area was for the motor heads and the grassy areas were for everyone!

Back in the day, you could take your car and drive thru the center of Dorney Park. This was also a big cruise spot on Sundays. Saturday nights, it was the stock car races at Dorney, a movie at a local theater or whatever you did on date night. There were also music concerts at Dorney Park. Castle garden was also a spot to go for dances, concerts and roller skating.

Where did we get our music? There were many outlets in the Valley. The most notable was Speedy's Record Shop at 6th & Hamilton Sts. They were the place to get all the new sounds in the 60's & early 70's. They carried at least the Top 100 45's and LP's. Other were The Record Shack at Lumber & Hamilton Sts that allowed you to buy and sell used records, Toones on Tilghman Street, Listening Booth in the Malls, Record City –Westgate, Whitehall Mall Records, Renaissance and Play It Again in Bethlehem. Titlow's also carried recorded music in the early years.

There was also a plethora of head shops and clothing shops in the area that catered to the needs of the 60's & 70's shoppers. These shops offered many items from Day-Glo posters to pipes to beads to tie-die shirts. It allowed the cool and hip among us to be fully supplied on all the neat items of the era. The Upper Story on Hamilton St was probably the best known shop of them all.

Phantasmagoria, Cinruss/Cinruss Garb in Allentown, Utopia in Easton were also a few other hip spots

Bands and DJ's looking to buy PA equipment usually went to the original Sight & Sound on 12th & Tilghman Sts and then on Hamilton Mall in Allentown. Also in Allentown were Lafayette Radio Electronics, Radio Shack and Eastern Light all on Hamilton St. Dave Phillips Music and Sound in Phillipsburg, NJ, Crest Wholesale Music, Titlow's, Kals Music in Whitehall, Georges in Northampton(local Fender franchise) and Kempfer Brothers were the spots for bands to shop for gear.

The Bandstand - 1984 Lehigh Parkway

When you got hungry, there was a host of places to stop for munchies, if you get my drift! Yocco's and Liberty Lunch on Liberty St and Marcos Hot Dogs had the best pups in town. For those in Phillipsburg, It was Jimmy's Hot Dogs on Union Square. You got a big pickle with each doggie. Georges Hoagie Shop near Muhlenberg College, Zandy's on the South Side at 8th & St John Sts and The Brass Rail at 12th & Hamilton or on Lehigh St, Vinces Steaks and of course, The Ritz Barbeque, were the top spots of the day. There were a couple of small greasy spoons around the area like Tommy's on 8th & Gordon and Moe's on New ST next to the Allen Theater. Bar food was plentiful throughout the Valley alsoat places like Sheiks, Stahley's and Cheers.

Movie theaters with single screens were a dime a dozen throughout the Valley. The Colonial, Rialto, Allen, Towne, Boyd, Strand, Capri, Eric, Franklin and 19th St Theaters in Allentown, The Roxy in Northampton, the Boyd in Bethlehem and The State in Easton all had the latest movies and matinees weekly. Also back then, we had the drive-in theater, the date night favorite for guys and girls. The West End, Boulevard, Shankweiler's and Becky's were the most popular and had music movies for the young set.

1 day outdoor festivals were also the rage back then. Super Sunday, which was held on the 3nd Sunday of September, in Allentown and the Bethlehem Art's on Main Street, which has been an annual event since 1965 is held on Mothers Day annually. Community Days in the smaller towns were held yearly. Fairs, carnivals and circuses were also a yearly summer ritual. Music had a big part in most of these festivals!

CHAPTER 12: LEHIGH VALLEY ROLL CALL

This chapter is dedicated to those performers, musicians, artists, media & support people from the area who played and worked in the Lehigh Valley, gave from the heart and left a their legacy on the Lehigh Valley area. The list keeps growing and we remember what these people did and how they left a lasting impression on all our lives.

**"If you believe in forever
Then life is just a one-night stand
If there's a rock and roll heaven
Well you know they've got a hell of a band"**

Bob Wolken – WGPA

Keith Smith – Roadie

Bob Gawlin – Sound Man

Scott Schneck aka Scott Hott

March 30th, 2009

Kelly Murphy

Jumpin Jay Sands – Morning Show DJ at WAEB AM 790

Bill Daniels – Rock Palace

Guy Randall Ackley -WAEB

Robert Hazard – singer

Sammy "Lugar" Rawhauser

Willie Restum

Rocco Mazzella – Tangier

Mario Perillo-Dead End Kids

Don Hunt (l) Service Electric

Carol Alee – Crisis

Billy Lomax – Dead End Kids

Les Paul

Larry Aranyos – WAEB, WODE

Joey Santangelo – Joey Saint

Tommy Carter – DEK

Tonya Brown – Queen Bee

Glenn Aranyos(r) PASCAL

Mark Klee "Mr Mark" WMUH

Tony Fasching – Kal's Kids

Mark Smitreski – Steeds

Candy Candido

Cheryl Dilcher – Singer

oey Mitchell-Snyder - RIP WEEX, WODE Oldies 99.9, WHTZ Hot 99.9, WQQQ - Q100

Harvey Banks & James"Otis"Nastasse

Mayor Daddona - music supporter

My mother Lois McKenna, who supported my efforts through the years, my aunt, Joyce Shellenberger, who wrote the Concert Schedule & Nightlife for the Morning Call from the mid 70's to 1990 and Arthur Lucier who was also of great support to me.

CHAPTER 13: LEHIGH VALLEY MUSIC PUBLICATIONS

The Lehigh Valley has been very fortunate indeed to have some independent music publications that were devoted almost entirely for original music and the bands that came from the Lehigh Valley area.

In the early 80's, PASCAL, the Pennsylvania Association of Songwriters, Composers & Lyricists published their own monthly magazine called the PASCAL Press. Under the guidance of PASCAL President John Havassy and Editor Bruce White, this local magazine became the definitive outlet for local bands and new acts to showcase their upcoming events and their material. The PASCAL Press lasted about 3 years before it was replaced by another publication.

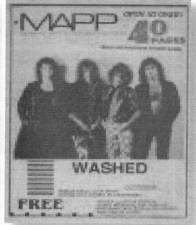

PASCAL Press   MAPP Magazine   Myself & Bruce White

Bruce White started another organization called Musicians, Artists, Poets, Performers & Songwriters (MAPPS) in the 1984 and published MAPPS magazine that covered the void left by the PASCAL press. The format was basically very similar to PP and was expanded in later years to cover a wider region of PA including Philadelphia and Western NJ.

The Aquarian Weekly is a regional alternative weekly newspaper based in New Jersey. Founded in 1969, its focus is popular music. It is accompanied by a pull-out section, The East Coast Rocker, which is freely distributed throughout the New Jersey/New York City/Eastern Pennsylvania region. The paper has remained independently owned and operated throughout its existence.

The Pennsylvania Musician has been in print for 28 years since 1982. The Pennsylvania Musician Magazine is designed as a publicity magazine for musicians, agents and clubs. The interest it has generated has sparked the renaissance of Pennsylvania's local entertainment scene. That in turn has made the Pennsylvania Musician the most informative and entertaining magazine in Pennsylvania. The PA Musician Magazine is a monthly publication and has a distribution of 15,000 per month.

The cover of the first issue

CREDITS

I would like to thank the following people for their contributions to this book. Without their assistance, this book would not be possible.

Dean Smith & Meg Vacchi-Smith from DSSmith Creative Group (DSSmithCreative.com) for the cover design and book layout. Frederick Jerant for the title of the book, Allentown Anglophile, Dave Peifly, City of Allentown, Jan & Tommy Zito, Steve & Kelly Molchany, Jimmy Alford, Larry Beahm, Richard Wolfe & The Roxy Theater, Wikipedia, Sam Younes, PASCAL, John Havassy, Valerie Chambers-Barber, Eric Geist, Bobby Scammell, Chuck Glendenmeyer, Daniel & Cindy Kocher, Manfred Kodilla, Tom & Bonnie Beier, Billy Daniels, Irwin Goldberg, Kevin Shire, Jeff Demko, Bob Rush, Mike Fox, Jim Loftus, JJ Sands, Bill Trousdale, Greg Roth, Chuck Hoerl, Angel Perez Hallman, Betsy Williams, Blake Dannen, Bob Weidner, Chuck Bachman, Cynthia & John Anglemeyer, Dave Fry, Davey Werkeiser, Diane Richter, Ron Sabol, Flamin Harry McGonigle, Scott Siska, Gloria Domina, Ian Bruce, Dave Bauder, Peter Noone, Hub Willson, Jerry Deane, Ken Matthews, Leslie West, Lisa Lake, Maureen "Moe" Jerant, Michelle Miatico McGee, Mitch Schecter, The Pa. Museum of Music and Broadcast History, Jay Thomas, Ron Sabol, Steve Brosky, John Cline, Susan Steele, Ken Siftar, The Goddess Brothers, Tony DiLeo, Rory Castellano, Chuck Glendenmeyer, Rick Levy, Al Check, Steve Valek, Craig Kastelnik, John Kacmarcik, Richie Unterberger, Paul Willistein, Sue Snyder, Aquarian Weekly, MAPPS, LV Rocks, Bruce White/Ian Bruce, Jack Burns – WALN, Mike Stengel, Joyce Shellenberger (RIP), all the bands, former and present band members listed in the book for their input, pictures and historical references and the photographers that took all the band glossys, all the concert venues, colleges and clubs listed in the book, local & regional radio stations, The Morning Call and to my many Facebook and MySpace friends who commented and contributed to my photo albums with many facts and photos that I was missing. All images have been used with expressed permission from the originators. I have made reasonable efforts to ensure that the information in this book is correct and to credit everyone who was involved in this undertaking…Thank you!